What people are saying about …

THE CHURCH OF FACEBOOK

"Jesse has a great mind and a wonderful voice. *The Church of Facebook* will help all of us understand community in deeper and better ways."

John Ortberg, author and pastor of
Menlo Park Presbyterian Church

"Through rich and compelling narrative, research, and examples, Jesse Rice educates us about the Higher Power behind virtual communities like Facebook and inspires us to become better people in this new era of human connectedness."

Clara Shih, creator of Faceconnector and author
of the best-selling book *The Facebook Era*

"Without understanding how technology is reshaping community and relationships we will not be effective leaders. Jesse raises excellent observations and provides hopeful ways to respond without cheapening what biblical community really is."

Dan Kimball, author of *They Like
Jesus but Not the Church*

"Jesse Rice's poignant thoughts on social networking come as a respected and thoughtful peer and not as someone who simply signed up for an account in an effort to research his next book. In *The Church of Facebook* Jesse Rice leads a much-needed conversation on virtual and actual community with wit, wisdom, and brilliant insight!"

"*The Church of Facebook* addresses the timely issue of how current technology is shaping the nature and quality of our relationships. By integrating the best of social psychology research with understated theological reflection, Jesse Rice guides us through this conversation in a way that is intensely readable, provocative, and engaging. With astute analysis and self-effacing wit, Rice gently helps us explore what it might mean to make a life in the way of Jesus amidst the complexity and newness of the online social-networking phenomenon."

"Weaving together the rigor of science, the wisdom of religion, and the insights of psychology, Jesse Rice presents an intentional, mindful, and authentic way of using Facebook. I hope that everyone involved in this virtual community reads the book!"

"The marriage of the two words *church* and *Facebook* seems akin to the collision between an immovable object and an unstoppable force, yet Jesse Rice skillfully navigates the potentially dangerous meeting. *The Church of Facebook* isn't just another anecdotal piece in the already busy and frenzied waters of social media and spirituality but adds a layer of discerning critique that can thankfully be applied to nearly all software applications and services on the Web today. The technological landscape in which we engage daily is changing whether we like it or not, and its effect and impact on us is extremely significant. Jesse discusses the obvious implications, elucidates those lesser (but no less important), and wades deep into the conversation."

John Saddington, senior editor
of ChurchCrunch.com

"As someone who constantly studies the ways Facebook is changing our lives and work, I can personally attest to the many benefits it and other new communication tools offer. However, as with any new technology, we must learn to wield it wisely and use it in life-giving ways. As part of an increasingly hyperconnected generation, it can be tempting to lose sight of the type of connection our souls truly desire. Jesse lovingly and prophetically reminds us that we were made for deep relationships, and that we must be mindful to engage with others on Facebook (and in every situation) with intentionality, humility, authenticity, and love. I'm very thankful Jesse wrote this book, and would recommend it enthusiastically to all."

Justin Smith, founder of Inside Facebook and
author of the best-selling *Facebook Marketing Bible*

"I have been waiting for years for Jesse to write this book. He is uniquely qualified and brings an insightful, humorous, and deep look at the issues of connection, community, the church, and the twenty-first century. Drawing from a wealth of eclectic sources, Jesse keeps the reader strongly engaged as he looks at the pervasive forces of humanity and technology and weaves together a powerful regenerative hope. I have already reread this book twice and have given copies away to many people. I hope you will too."

Nancy Ortberg, author of *Looking for God: An Unexpected Journey Through Tattoos, Tofu, and Pronouns*

"Jesse Rice takes his readers on a journey through the ever-shifting landscape of virtual community with fresh insight and warm candor. But Facebook junkies and critics alike, beware: *The Church of Facebook* will also shed light on what may be keeping you from the kind of relationships your heart most desires."

Scott Scruggs, teaching pastor at Menlo Park Presbyterian Church

THE CHURCH OF
facebook®

THE CHURCH OF
facebook®

How the Hyperconnected Are
Redefining Community

JESSE RICE

THE CHURCH OF FACEBOOK
Published by David C. Cook
4050 Lee Vance View
Colorado Springs, CO 80918 U.S.A.

David C. Cook Distribution Canada
55 Woodslee Avenue, Paris, Ontario, Canada N3L 3E5

David C. Cook U.K., Kingsway Communications
Eastbourne, East Sussex BN23 6NT, England

David C. Cook and the graphic circle C logo
are registered trademarks of Cook Communications Ministries.

The Web site addresses recommended throughout this book are offered as a
resource to you. These Web sites are not intended in any way to be or imply an
endorsement on the part of David C. Cook, nor do we vouch for their content.

Scripture taken from the HOLY BIBLE, TODAY'S NEW
INTERNATIONAL VERSION®. Copyright © 2001, 2005 by Biblica®.
Used by permission of Biblica®. All rights reserved worldwide.
The author has added italics to Scripture quotations and quoted material for emphasis.

LCCN 2009932745
ISBN 978-1-4347-6534-5
eISBN 978-1-4347-0066-7

© 2009 Jesse Rice

The Team: Andrea Christian, Nicci Hubert, Amy
Kiechlin, Jaci Schneider, and Karen Athen
Cover Design: Rule 29
Cover Images: iStockphoto, royalty free

Printed in the United States of America
First Edition 2009

2 3 4 5 6 7 8 9 10

010510

For Mom.

CONTENTS

INTRODUCTION

Imagine that it's a typically brisk but sunny day in London and, bundled up appropriately against the chill (and with your tiny digital camera in hand), you're touring around some of the many famous sites the city has to offer. You've just passed through beautiful St. Paul's Cathedral and you're kicking yourself for not coming yesterday; admission is free on Sundays, after all, and you're on a tight budget. You step out of the massive domed neoclassical building onto the northern bank of the Thames River, opening up your map of central London as you do. Scanning it as the edges flap in the breeze, you notice that just across the Thames from St. Paul's is the Tate Modern Gallery. The Tate is home to some of the finest modern art in the world despite the fact that it looks like a giant industrial barn where one might milk several thousand cows. You decide it would be interesting to see what the gallery has to offer, and with the raucous sounds of a busy London Monday buzzing in your ears, you look up from your map and across to the other side of the river. And without taking another step, you realize exactly how you're going to get from here to there.

The Millennium Bridge opened in June 2000, and it is a work of the finest thought and craftsmanship. It was the first pedestrian footbridge to be constructed across the Thames in central London in more than a hundred years, and it cost just over twenty million pounds to build.[1] The bridge's architect, Sir Norman Foster, had been a fan of Flash Gordon comic books as a kid, and drew on some of his memories of Flash when first imagining the bridge's design. Foster recalled that, when Flash needed to get around from place to place in order to save the world, he would hold out his hand and extend something that looked like a Jedi's light saber to create a "blade of light" upon which he could cross over from one point to another. As you stow your map and start making your way across what has now officially become known as "The Blade of Light," you begin to understand Foster's intention in creating much more than just a functional bridge. You're also delighted to find there is no toll for crossing.

The bridge itself is highly unusual in its design, and one of the first things you observe midway across is the view. Your view of the Thames is almost completely unhindered by traditional suspension cables, the fruit of a two-hundred-person design and engineering team that labored in earnest for several years to realize Foster's vision. Rather than the support cables

---

1 Please see the bibliography in the back of this book for the books and articles I use as references in each chapter.

that hang down in a reversed arc that you'd typically find on a suspension bridge (San Francisco's Golden Gate is a perfect example), the Millennium Bridge's cables are tucked on the side and underneath, appearing as "wings" that fly along the length of the bridge. The entire steel structure is four meters wide (about twelve feet) and almost three hundred and thirty meters long (just over three football fields), making it the sleekest suspension bridge in the world. Unlike anything seen before, it was truly an engineering masterpiece.

Or so it seemed to everyone on the dawn of opening day.

June 10, 2000, marked the grand opening of the Millennium Bridge, and thousands of people gathered early to be among the first to travel across its span. The large team that had designed, built, tested, refined, and retested every last detail of the bridge beamed with pride. All of London seemed to hold its breath as the ribbon was ceremoniously cut, and the cheering throng stepped onto the bridge. A dozen news reporters, multiple film crews, and every last person with a tiny digital camera like yours captured what happened next. And what happened next was the very thing that immediately shut down the brand-new Millennium Bridge.

As the crowd advanced over the bridge, the combination of all the footsteps from pedestrians sent a distinct vibration throughout the structure. Each wholly random step from each entirely different individual produced a certain amount of energy that spread and began to synchronize across the entire span of the bridge. This synchronized pattern continued until the whole structure began to sway and bend from side to side, wobbling like the blade of an old metal saw. In order for the crowd to keep from toppling over onto one another and to continue forward movement across the bridge, each person had to begin to waddle unnaturally, taking wide steps out and to the right, then out and to the left, and so on—what one participant later referred to as a "skating gait." Very quickly the entire crowd was stepping in the same way at exactly the same time. Just like the vibrations in the bridge, the pedestrians also became synchronized. Still photos and video footage from the event convey what looked like an inebriated but unified group procession down a wedding aisle or, more precisely, a choreographed ice-skating show. Of course, this "choreographed" movement only exacerbated the problem, creating more wave-generating energy and compounding the swaying effect until the whole structure became totally unstable.

The media went wild, immediately dubbing the Millennium Bridge a flop. Some masterpiece of engineering, they jeered. "It was like being on a boat," reported one shaken pedestrian. Another expressed shock that "we all had to conform to the movement of the bridge." The design team, composed of some of the most brilliant engineering minds from around the world, was forced to admit it had never imagined the outcome that surprised everyone on opening day, despite endless testing and reworking. "I was a little disappointed," said the lead engineer in typical understated British style. "We had worked really hard to sort out all the details." The freshly minted pride of London was shut down for repairs almost as soon as it had opened for business. It would have remained a bulky hunk of steel uselessly across two empty water bottles that were placed on their sides in parallel to one another and a few inches apart. When viewed from the front, the contraption looked like a pontoon boat of questionable seaworthiness. Next, Strogatz placed two matching metronomes atop either end of the notebook. He then started the metronomes ticking at the same tempo, but out of sync with each other, which resulted in making the whole creation wobble slightly from side to side. For a few moments nothing seemed to happen except for the wholly random ticking sound of the metronomes. Then suddenly the audience noticed a shift. In fact they could *hear* the shift even before they saw it. "The metronomes," Strogatz explained, "are 'speaking' to each other." He went on to clarify that each metronome was responding to the motion the other generated across the surface of the notebook as it rested on the water bottles. They were each "communicating" their individual timing to the other, allowing them to line up rhythmically. Within a few more seconds the two inanimate metronomes fell into sync with one another, ticking away harmoniously as the audience murmured with delighted surprise.

Strogatz went on to share with his entrepreneurial audience an example of "sync" from the world of biology. He showed video footage shot at night that captured male fireflies trying to attract a mate in the mangrove trees of places like Thailand and Borneo. The fireflies (that are actually beetles) used their self-generated on-off light to draw the attention of passing females. As a species, Strogatz pointed out, they have developed the capacity to do this in partnership with one another to compound the seductive effect. Rather than just a single flashbulb to call the ladies over, the males work as a team—in sync—to capture the attention of as many females as possible. After all, the fireflies assume, the more women, the better the chances (this is also the assumption, though ill-founded, of most eighteen-year-old boys). The results as seen on film look like something from the Disney Electric Light Parade as thousands of male fireflies flash on and off again and again as though every tree on the river banks were decorated with synchronized blinking Christmas lights. The effect is so stunning that it initially baffled early researchers, several claiming it was merely a trick of the eyes or some other human misperception.

While his audience watched in wonder, Steven Strogatz summarized his case for the prevalence of synchronicity at every level of nature, with examples from the subatomic to the farthest reaches of the universe. He pointed out more obvious examples like fish that move in schools and birds that travel in flocks. He tied in our human experience, as well. "We [humans] actually take pleasure in synchronicity," said Strogatz. "We sing together. We dance together." In fact, while he conceded the law of entropy that proves objects both animate and inanimate typically move toward disorder, he also claimed that the tendency toward the harmonization of objects might be an even more certain reality. "*Sync,*" Strogatz says, "might be the most pervasive force in nature."

In light of what we've learned about spontaneous order, let's return now to the opening day of London's Millennium Bridge. Three "realities" factor prominently into the story. The first reality is that the events on the Millennium Bridge indicate, as Strogatz suggests, some powerful and "pervasive force" that can spontaneously synchronize both animate and inanimate objects. *Something* set the bridge in motion and fostered its shaky development into a full-blown carnival ride. The second reality is that the events of opening day produced results that no one could have predicted—not even the brightest engineering minds in the world. Despite strict testing and retesting, despite taking every precaution and probing every potential downfall, the bridge responded on opening day in a way that no one could have foreseen. And the third reality is that the results produced by the unanticipated onset of spontaneous order demanded that the crowd traversing the bridge had to adapt their behavior significantly in order to accommodate the changing conditions. They had to quickly learn to walk in step in order to safely navigate the shifting bridge underfoot.

To put it even more simply, in the example of the Millennium Bridge, we find these three realities at work:

1. There is a force that is capable of synchronizing a large population in very little time, thereby creating spontaneous order.

2. This spontaneous order can generate outcomes that are entirely new and unpredictable.

3. These unpredictable outcomes require the affected population to adapt their behavior to
more adequately live within the new spontaneously generated order.

What we are about to learn in the course of this book is
that these three realities parallel exactly the lightning-quick rise
and radical pervasiveness of the cultural phenomenon known
as Facebook. Reflecting the three realities, this book is divided
into three sections. In the first section we will discover the
"force" or gravity that has pulled hundreds of millions of users
into Facebook's orbit in only five short years, the vast majority
of whom have arrived in just the past eighteen months. In the
second section we will investigate the new and unexpected outcomes of our social-networking habits—the good, the bad, and
the downright confusing—that result when our brilliant but
imperfect humanity collides headlong with Facebook's brilliant
but imperfect technology.

Finally, in the third section we will explore the types of
adaptation that will best help us navigate the shifting social
tides, learning as we go how to enrich our relationships and
better understand ourselves in the process.

Because this book also contains a spiritual thread woven
throughout,[2] much of the discussion will be framed with biblical insights. In no way is this approach intended as a means
for selling a particular kind of faith or doctrine. Everyone has

---

2 See title of book for more information.

their own understanding and experience of faith, and *all* are welcome into the conversation found here. It is simply my contention that the gospel (literally, "good news") of Jesus is particularly well suited for helping us understand, adapt to, and even thrive among the challenges of living within a hyperconnected culture.

And now, to begin our investigation, we must travel to a place from whence many tall tales have emerged: the white-sand beaches of the Mexican Riviera.

There is a force that is capable of synchronizing a large population in very little time, thereby creating spontaneous order.

ONE
CONNECTION

Akumal, Mexico, is just over an hour south of Cancun on the Mexican Riviera, a quaint resort community surrounded by white sandy beaches and lush jungle palms. Its miniscule "downtown" is composed of two small grocery stores, half a dozen restaurants, and a scuba-diving shop. It is positioned on a long stretch of beach regarded for its snorkeling and giant sea turtles. It is a tourist trap but few tourists know of it, keeping life in Akumal consistently vibrating at little more than a soothing hum. In other words, it is paradise.

On New Years Day 1998, three particularly pasty psychologists found themselves luxuriating in Akumal while discussing the topic, "What makes people happy?" As soft, eighty-degree breezes swept over the tops of their little tropical drinks sporting little tropical umbrellas, it was difficult to imagine discussing anything else.

Renown psychologist Martin Seligman was one of the three. His round, clean-shaven face and mostly bald head framed an easy smile, making him look like a beardless Santa Claus with a badly sunburned nose. Together with Ray Fowler and Mihaly Csikszentmihalyi (yes, that's a lot of consonants but it's easily pronounced: "cheeks-sent-me-high"), he was celebrating his very first day as president of the American Psychological Association. Seligman was known around the world for his work studying learned helplessness, depression, and, conversely, for his founding contributions to the emerging field of positive psychology. Each incoming APA president is asked to choose a theme for their yearlong term of office. Seligman, frustrated that so much of his field seemed entirely focused on the broken parts of humanity, wanted to steer things in a more optimistic direction. Thus the quiet beach resort, thus the tropical drinks, and thus the question, "What makes people happy?"

One year after that very conversation, Seligman and company—plus a group of young talent being groomed to lead the charge for a more optimistic approach in their field—returned to Akumal as part of a first annual conference on "positive psychology." The tiny beach community had never seen so much pale skin. Not that psychology had always turned a blind eye to optimism. Throughout the decades there had always been a few rogues willing to brave their fellow researchers' suspicious looks and folded arms in order to promote a more positive approach to well-being. But here was the beginning of a movement to reorient the entire field, to mainstream what had until then seemed little more than a fringe curiosity.

In the years following the conference, the evidence for what makes people happy began to roll in like a gentle wave in Akumal. What did researchers find? You may be surprised.

More money doesn't make you happy. Yes, we've all been told that "money can't buy happiness," but here for the first time was actual scientific research that showed, once our basic material needs are met, additional income does almost nothing to raise our sense of satisfaction with life. (Wouldn't we all love the chance to prove the exception to the rule?) How about education? Would another degree at a better institution make me happy? Again, research showed that more or better education or even a higher IQ did not equate to happiness. How about the quest to remain eternally young? In a culture that has elevated adolescence into an art form, surely perpetual youth would make us happy? Not so fast. Older people, studies revealed, were consistently happier than younger people. They were also less prone to bouts of depression. What about sunny weather? Be honest: Aren't Californians happier than Michiganders? Research suggested that while those surveyed in the Midwest assumed Californians were a happier bunch thanks to their extra dose of vitamin D, it turns out there is no correlation between balmy weather and consistent feelings of well-being (though after a long Portland, Oregon, winter, my in-laws usually beg to differ).

So what *does* cause happiness? Dr. Edward Diener—known to his associates as "Dr. Happiness"—conducted a 2002 study along with Martin Seligman at the University of Illinois. That particular study summed up much of positive psychology's overall findings. Students who tested with the highest levels of happiness and the fewest signs of depression all had one foundational thing in common: significant social ties to friends and family.

In other words, *connection* is the key to happiness.

"Authentic connection," writes psychologist Janet L. Surrey, "is described as the core of psychological wellbeing and is the essential quality of growth-fostering and healing relationships. In moments of deep connection in relationship, we break out of isolation and contraction into a more whole and spacious state of mind and heart."

At the root of human existence is our great need for connection: connection with one another, with our own hearts and minds, and with a loving God who intended intimate connection with us from the beginning. Connection is the very core of what makes us human and the very means by which we express our humanity. As Surrey notes, there are no "growth-fostering" or "healing" relationships without connection. Apart from its presence the human heart becomes isolated and fragmented. Let's look more closely at the power of connection through the lens of two compelling stories.

Harry Frederick Harlow was born October 31, 1905. His parents were Mabel Rock and Alonzo Harlow *Israel*. Harry Harlow was not Jewish, but as an adult he changed his original surname from "Israel" to "Harlow" because he feared the prejudice he likely would have encountered in academic circles of the 1940s and '50s. In grade school and throughout high school, Harlow demonstrated great proficiency in English, so when he headed off to university, he naturally chose English as his major. Harlow spent his first year studying at Reed College in Oregon and then transferred to Stanford University. At Stanford, Harlow continued his studies, but to his surprise, began doing very poorly in his English courses. Partly to avoid flunking out of Stanford and partly due to a growing interest in human behavior, Harlow switched his studies to psychology. Small decisions can make a big difference. Harlow's decision to switch majors would eventually revolutionize the entire field of psychology.

Harlow completed both his undergraduate and doctoral degrees at Stanford, taking a professorship at the University of Wisconsin almost as soon as he removed his graduation gown. It was at Wisconsin that Harlow would make a name for himself in a series of cleverly designed experiments that involved a seemingly endless supply of rhesus monkeys.

Harlow, who looked exactly like what you'd expect from a research scientist in the 1950s—white lab coat, horn-rimmed glasses, grease-slicked black hair—was interested in *love*. In fact his name eventually became synonymous with the "science of affection," and his best-known paper was titled, "The

Nature of Love." Harlow's fellow researchers often heckled him and dismissed his fascination with affection for not being "scientific enough." But he wasn't deterred. Love was on Harlow's mind and he knew it was on most other minds as well.

Interestingly, Harlow's own romantic life would itself become a laboratory of love. He met his first wife, Clara, while she was a subject in a famous IQ study that Harlow just happened to be helping to administer. Clara posted a whopping 150 on the IQ test—well into the "genius" category. They were married in 1932 and had two children, Robert and Richard. Harlow and Clara later divorced in 1946. One year later Harlow remarried. His new wife, Margaret, was herself a bright psychologist. Together, they had two more children, Pamela and Jonathan. Sadly, Margaret died in 1970 after a long battle with cancer. Again just a single year passed before Harlow was married once more. What kind of brilliant mind did he choose to wed this time? To everyone's surprise Harlow *remarried* his first wife, Clara. They lived out the rest of their days together until 1981 when Harlow passed away. Hollywood screenwriters have written less interesting love stories.

But all of that lay in the future. For now, as a professor at the University of Wisconsin, Harlow's primary "romantic interest" was in primates. One experiment in particular put Harlow on the map. Curious how infant rhesus monkeys would behave in an artificial environment, Harlow and his team built two artificial monkey "mothers." The first was constructed of simple wire mesh and had a blank-faced head screwed on the top with a tube running out from its neck that could deliver milk to the infant monkey. It resembled the kind of demonic stick figure that people typically ignite at the end of the annual Burning Man festival. The second "mother" was identical except that its "face" was more monkeylike, and its wire mesh frame was covered with soft, warm terrycloth. It looked like an elongated furry snowman that would like to be everyone's friend. There was one more key distinction between the two mothers: The cloth-covered contraption did not have a feeding tube. It was incapable of providing the infant monkey with food.

The black-and-white film from Harlow's experiment is both hilarious and heartbreaking to watch. As the tiny elflike monkeys stumble around their cages just a few days after birth, they quickly climb up and take a sip from the *wire* mother but then scramble immediately back to the *cloth* mother, where they spend the vast majority of their day. If any element of fear was introduced into the environment, as was the case when researchers placed a drum-playing toy bear into their cage (and who wouldn't find such a thing troubling?), the little monkeys always ran to the *cloth* mother for comfort instead of the food-dispensing wire mother, clinging to her with all their strength until the fear passed.

Harlow and his team had expected the infant monkeys to create some kind of "bond" between mother and child immediately following birth. What they did not anticipate was, if forced to choose, the monkeys would select the nonfeeding cloth mother over the food-delivering wire mother every time. Their need for comforting connection, it seemed, was even greater than their need for food!

But there was more. Following his initial discoveries, Harlow introduced a series of modifications to his experiment. In one case he took away the choice between monkey mothers by separating the infants into two different environments: one with only a wire mother and one with only a cloth mother (a tube was added to the cloth mother to support feeding). Harlow found that monkeys from either environment developed physically at the same rate. It appeared there was little or no difference in the "connective effects" of cloth or wire. This seemed to imply that *what* the monkeys were connected to did not really matter. The only important thing was that they had some kind of connection.

But the scary drum-playing toy bear changed all of that. When the mechanical bear was placed in the "cloth" cages, the frightened monkeys would scramble on to the cloth mother, cuddling and rubbing against her until they were at last able to calm themselves. At that point, the monkeys would relax and even become curious and playful about sharing a cage with a toy bear, venturing away from the cloth mother in brief excursions to sniff and paw at it.

The monkeys in the "wire" cages, however, could not have responded more differently. When the menacing toy bear was introduced into the wire cages, the little monkeys fell to pieces. They threw themselves on the floor, and rocked back and forth. They screamed in terror. The effect is so dramatic that footage from the experiment can be quite disturbing to watch.[1]

What Harlow concluded was that the monkeys in the "cloth" cages must have had access to some kind of psychological resource—what he later called *emotional attachment*—to help them deal with challenges in their environment, especially the introduction of fear. The monkeys in the "wire" cages had no such resources and fell apart at the first sign of danger. This, Harlow began to see, was evidence that there was in fact a certain *kind* of connection important not only to healthy development but also to serve in adequately facing challenges that might appear.

Harlow found that there are indeed different types of connection that make for different types of responses. There are some types of connection that enable adaptation and resiliency. There are other connections that create psychological breakdown. The monkeys from either cage developed physically at normally expected rates. They appeared to be identically healthy and normal from the outside. And they behaved as you would expect healthy monkeys to behave. But those similarities vanished the moment some change—especially some *threat*—was introduced into their environment. When that happened, the difference in their "inner" realities became obvious. One kind of connection had led to the inner strength necessary to cope

---

1 Harlow came under fire for his experiments with rhesus monkeys. Few, if any, of his experiments would likely be allowed today. Ironically, however, the ethical treatment of animals movement finds its roots in Harlow's studies, as does much of our current understanding and treatment of children with backgrounds of abuse and neglect. An example of his work can be seen at http://www.youtube.com/watch?v=fLrBrk9DXVk.

with and even overcome environmental changes. The other had led to inner chaos and a radically diminished capacity to cope with anything at all.

Harlow's findings reflect what we now know to be true for human babies, as well. *Bonding*, the psychological process by which a mother creates a safe and nurturing environment for the child to develop, lays the groundwork for the baby's ability to grow into a healthy and well-adapted adult. That is why, as soon as is possible, the new mother is handed her fresh-out-of-the-womb baby to physically bond with. If a physical connection is not possible—for example, a health issue that requires the baby to initially be kept in an incubator—mothers are encouraged to speak tenderly to their child, connecting and intimately bonding through the soothing tones of their own voice. Studies have shown that, just like the little rhesus monkeys, a human baby's need to bond with its parent may be even more important than its need for food.[2]

Harlow's findings revolutionized the way psychologists thought about human relationships. Until then it was unlikely any scientist in his right mind would have claimed that some kind of emotional connection was more important to a growing infant than the most basic of all needs, food. But what Harlow demonstrated so vividly with infant monkeys, and what study after study has shown to be all the more true in human beings, is that connection is not just "what causes happiness." It is also our most basic need.

---

2 Admittedly other studies have shown that feeding your baby is still a good idea.

The reality of our innate need for connection is often most clearly revealed in the experience of *dis*-connection. Dropped cell phone calls, the loss of a job or career opportunity, a romantic breakup, the death of a loved one—each kind of disconnection alerts us to the fact that we were meant to connect. The feelings that result from a broken connection can run the gamut from simple frustration to complete personal devastation. But we need not explore something as painful as death in order to further illustrate the effects of disconnection. We can do something as simple as turning on the "telly."

The BBC, the United Kingdom's mammoth media empire, produces some of the most clever and thought-provoking programming that often tickles the funny bone while stretching the intellect. And no, I'm not talking about *The Office*. In 2006 a BBC television series called *Horizon* invited six people to take part in a compelling experiment. Adam, Claire, Rickey, Judy, Barney, and Bill agreed to subject themselves to forty-eight hours of sensory deprivation. They signed up to be "disconnected" in every way in order to see what would happen.

Adam is a stand-up comedian in his late twenties. He has a significantly receding hairline, a slight paunch in his belly, and eyes that appear slightly crossed. He's the most extroverted of the six, a person who—like most extroverts—requires a great deal of sensory stimulation to make sense of the world. He jokes self-effacingly as he imagines the toll the next two days will take on him. "I'm afraid I'll go mad. What if I start smashing things up?"

Claire is also in her late twenties with short dark hair and a pretty smile. She says she likes a challenge. "I do try to push myself." As a doctoral student in psychology, she seems ideally suited to thrive in an experiment where her mind will be put to the test.

Bill looks lean and strong and is a former ad executive. He is the oldest in the bunch. He plans to cope with the forty-eight hour experiment by using his skills in meditation. "Every day I like to spend time on my own. I sometimes fantasize about being a hermit, about living up in the mountains and coming down to buy a few supplies in town, then going back to my cabin." If anyone is going to be fine after two days without human connection, it seems to be Bill.

Rickey is a thirtysomething postal worker whose primary hobby is running one-hundred-mile ultramarathons. Yes, you read that correctly—*one hundred miles*. He plans to think of the experiment as just another test of his endurance.

Barney is a film archivist who imagines quietly that he will probably have a hard time over the next two days.

Judy is a copywriter for a toy manufacturer. "I'm very excited to get started," Judy says, not sounding too excited at all. "I don't know how I'm going to last, but I guess I'll just keep going."

As you can see, the "*Horizon* Six" were not extraordinary people, at least not any more extraordinary than the rest of us.[3] They all had their own ideas of how to best handle a situation like this and their own concerns about whether those techniques would actually work. They were average folks who simply wanted to put themselves to the test, to see what would happen when they were disconnected from life as they normally experienced it.

The experiment took place in an abandoned nuclear bunker, the kind of dark and creepy place straight out of a Hollywood horror film. Walking down the stairs and into the long, dimly lit halls of the concrete structure, one might expect to stumble upon a cast of overly attractive twentysomethings being systematically stalked and hacked to death by some very disturbed but strangely likeable assailant.

The six subjects were given a battery of tests to use for before-and-after comparisons. In the first test, they were given a letter—F, for example—then asked to think of as many words as possible in one minute that began with that letter. Classic Adam: "Fake, farting, football ..." For the most part, each of the six breezes through, listing dozens of words that begin with F, though no one else seems to come up with anything as creative as a "fake, farting, football." The next test is presented to them. In this one the subjects are handed a sheet of paper. On the paper are the names of colors printed in columns: black, red, green, etc. But here's the catch: The names of the colors

---

3 Okay, maybe ultramarathon-runner Rickey is a wee bit more extraordinary than most of us. I mean, really? One hundred miles? And here's a random question: If the *Horizon* Six were in a fight with the Oceanic Six, who would come out on top? Let's keep it interesting—what if Jack only used one arm and Kate didn't bring a gun?

do not match the actual color of the ink with which they were printed. For example, the word "black" was actually printed in green ink, the word "red" was printed in black ink, and so on. The subjects are then asked to name the color of ink with which each color's name was printed. It's trickier than you think. Our brains typically register a printed word before we register the color of the printed word. But with a little bit of thought, each subject does quite well. They moved on to the final test. While the researchers were curious how the subjects would perform on the first two tests—any drops in performance would be easy to measure when everything was over—they were secretly interested in something quite different.

The last test, the one the researchers were most interested in, measured "levels of suggestibility." What they wanted to find out was just how vulnerable someone might become to the power of suggestion when they are cut off from connection, disconnected from their social and sensory worlds. Would they fall for a lie? Would they give in to someone else's point of view even if it were clearly "wrong"? To test for suggestibility, the researchers read their subjects a story with lots of intricate details, then quizzed them. "Was the assailant hit with a fist or a handbag?" Claire is asked. She looks at the researcher with a furrowed brow. "Well, neither." Claire gets it right. They were trying to pull one over on her, but she was alert for the details. In fact all of the men and women in the group tested fairly well in the first round. In other words, they had very low levels of suggestibility and could not be talked into believing something that wasn't true.

With the testing behind them, the *Horizon* Six were placed into tiny individual concrete rooms with nothing but a lonely bed for furniture. The rooms looked very much like prison cells without toilets.[4] Three of the subjects were placed in rooms completely sealed off from any light source; they could not see their hands in front of their faces. The other three were placed in well-lit rooms, but it came with a catch. They were stuffed into large, padded gloves and socks to disrupt their sense of touch, frosted goggles to completely hinder their vision, and headphones that played nothing but white noise to thwart their hearing. (The gloves were later removed when the subjects complained of painful rashes.)

As the experiment finally got under way, Claire was immediately overwhelmed by the inky blackness of her cell. She anxiously relayed to her observers that her bed sheets were cold and wet and that something should be done immediately to remedy the situation. Intending to remain silent so as not to influence any outcomes, her observers acquiesced to her concern and assured her via intercom that she was mistaken. The sheets were not wet, they said. She was just imagining things. "I don't think you're taking my concerns about the blankets very seriously," Claire lamented. "No one should have to sleep in wet sheets." After a short time Claire gave up trying to convince them and climbed into a fetal position on her bed.

---

4 *Horizon* failed to explain how the subjects used the bathroom during their two-day stay. Had I been a subject in the same experiment, that would have been my very first question.

After just nine hours the subjects were showing signs of wear. "I'm finding this grossly boring," said Barney. Adam echoed Barney's thoughts: "It's unbearable. I can feel my brain not wanting to do anything." Adam's statement may not be far from what actually happens during solitary confinement and sensory deprivation. Just as new neural pathways form in our brain as a result of stimulation, there is now research to show that the opposite may also true. If the brain does not get the stimulation it needs, it begins to turn to mush. Bill, who seemed so keen to spend time by himself in the beginning, now complained, "I don't really want to be here. It's starting to get on my nerves. I feel like a … helpless lab rat." Claire was found in her "cell" counting to herself. Barney had taken up singing. Judy, in the meantime, had simply fallen asleep.

After twenty-four hours (or the time it takes Jack Bauer to save Los Angeles from imminent destruction), the subjects began to exhibit truly bizarre behavior. They raised their voices in angry complaint to the walls. They wept uncontrollably. Many experienced vivid hallucinations. Adam reported, "I thought I could see a pile of oyster shells, empty, to represent all the nice food I could have eaten inside here." Poor Claire was suffering similar effects. "There's a snake there," she said, pointing to the floor. In another strange visual display of the effects of disconnection, almost all the subjects began to pace their tiny rooms back and forth, their brains working to self-generate some kind of stimulation in order to keep them going. Not Judy, of course. Judy was still asleep. Judy's eternal sleep, it turned out, was simply her body and mind's way of dealing with the overwhelming lack of connection, just another form of a coping mechanism.

After forty hours Adam was in tears. "This is close to insanity." The subjects seemed to have plummeted in both cognitive and behavioral functioning. Barney was singing again—poorly. Most had begun "hearing things," and claimed that "someone seemed to be in the room" with them. Judy was—you guessed it—still sleeping.

Finally, the experiment came to a close. A researcher's voice broke through the inky silence in each of their cells, causing them all a fright. "The forty-eight hours are over." Adam cried out for relief: "I just want to kiss the person who's letting me out!" Bill was similarly thrilled and laughed to himself. Claire was visibly relieved. Judy mumbled sleepily, "Oh. Excellent."

But before they could be reconnected to the outside world, the subjects were readministered the same battery of tests they were given at the beginning in order to reveal any cognitive changes resulting from their two days as lab rats. Of course, almost without exception, everyone performed poorly, further proving the disabling effects of isolation (as if anyone needed more evidence than the video footage captured in each subject's room[5]). Finally, the camera followed each of the six as they walked back through long, dark halls, up the tall steel stairs, and finally out into the sunshine. Adam, Claire, Rickey, Judy,

---

5 When the test measuring levels of "suggestibility" was readministered to the six, there was a surprising result. It was expected that all would suffer quite a bit from the effects of the previous forty-eight hours, but the women actually tested significantly better than the men. In fact they showed no change in suggestibility at all. Not so the men, who could seemingly be talked into anything during the final exam.

Barney, and Bill were elated to be set free into a world brimming with connection. "My senses are overwhelmed by the sights, sounds, and smells," said Adam. "You have no idea how good this feels."

BBC's *Horizon* experiment revealed two natural results of disconnection that illustrate our human need to connect. The first result: Cut off from connection, our ability to make sense of the world begins to break down. We begin to see things that aren't there, to buy into a reality that is wholly skewed. There were no snakes slithering on Claire's floor. Neither were her sheets wet and cold. They were dry and room temperature, the same as everyone else's. And Adam did not really have a large pile of seashells growing at the foot of his bed. His room was as empty as the rest. In the real world—the world of connection—Claire and Adam were normally adjusted human beings. In the experimental world—the world of disconnection—they became hallucinating paranoids.

The second result demonstrated by the *Horizon* experiment was that, cut off from connection, our ability to cope with reality quickly dissolves. In just one day of sensory deprivation and social isolation, each subject was reduced to infantile and even animalistic behavior. They cried uncontrollably and talked to themselves out loud. They rolled up into fetal positions and huddled on their beds. They yelled at the unsympathetic walls of their room. They even paced their constricting cages like jungle animals, waiting for the moment to attack and escape. Apparently baby rhesus monkeys aren't the only mammals that fall apart without the proper connection.

Obviously, the six subjects in the *Horizon* experiment were placed in extraordinary circumstances. Not many of us (hopefully) live in tiny concrete rooms dominated by an absence of sight, sound, and touch. But the experiment proved what Martin Seligman and his associates began to uncover on the beaches of Akumal, demonstrating its truth by revealing its opposite: If connection can make us happy, then disconnection can make us unhappy. No matter how it was tested, though, connectedness *mattered.*

Two stories, one common thread woven throughout: the inestimable power of connection. As we saw with Harlow and his monkeys, connection lays the groundwork for growth. In connection we find comfort and safety. We find a nurturing space that allows us to develop as a whole person, maturing inwardly even as we develop outwardly. Without it we might fall apart in the face of terrifying teddy bears. But in the presence of connection, the same toy bear—or whatever real-world challenge we might face—can become a mere curiosity, something we simply adapt to and overcome, growing stronger as we do.

The *Horizon* Six echoed Harlow's research: Apart from connection we fall to pieces. Our physical, emotional, and cognitive powers weaken significantly. We become vulnerable to suggestion, and can be easily led to believe things that aren't true. Our decision-making ability gets cloudy. Our way of viewing the

world becomes skewed. We question our ability to cope: Are
we going crazy? Will we be able to make it? Am I truly alone?
Disconnection seems to leave us locked in little rooms with no
light source and no sense of when the madness will end. But it
also reminds us of how precious connection truly is. Remember
how the subjects responded when finally released from captivity,
when they were finally reconnected to their natural environment? Adam, the highly extroverted stand-up comedian, said
it best: "You have no idea how good this feels." Connection, it
seems, makes all the difference.

Of course, we are talking about a certain *quality* of connection,
aren't we? Not just any connection can keep someone from falling to pieces. The average television satellite dish connects us to
two hundred-plus channels, each with its own endless number
of programs. But not many of us can claim that such a wide
variety of connections has revolutionized our lives. Clearly not
just any connection will do.

We can look to our own life experience as evidence in the
case for quality versus quantity. There are certain people whose
emails and phone calls we answer right away, and certain other
people whose emails and phone calls we don't answer at all. If
we are having a particularly difficult day, questioning our own
worth, wondering what is the point in going on with life, we
tend to share this with a certain *kind* of person and not necessarily the young man behind the counter of our nearest gas

station.[6] Similarly, if we have good news to share—if a wedding is proposed or a baby is on its way—celebration is usually all the more rich when communicated to certain favorite people.

If we are to make sense of why certain kinds of connection are beneficial and certain others aren't, we must be more precise in our definition of "connection." We have to get clear on what *kind* of connection has the power to secure, grow, free, and transform us. Toward the beginning of this chapter, I quoted psychologist Janet L. Surrey. Here she is again.

> *Authentic connection is described as the core of psychological wellbeing and is the essential quality of growth-fostering and healing relationships. In moments of deep connection in relationship, we break out of isolation and contraction into a more whole and spacious state of mind and heart.*

Surrey uses words like "authentic" and "deep" to convey the type of connection that is powerful enough to break us out of "isolation and contraction into a more whole and spacious state of mind and heart." Even though "authentic" and "deep" are

---

6 While confession to your local gas station attendant seems silly at first, there is growing evidence to support the idea that confession—in any form and to any person—is a healthy and redemptive experience. That's the claim of many who use GroupHug, one of dozens of Web sites that have invited people to own up to their misdeeds and apologize for the world to hear. Users reveal everything from cheating on a test to cheating on a spouse (and everything between and beyond). They can also get "hugs" from other users as a means of emotional support. The response has been impressive. Since GroupHug's founding in 2003, several hundred thousand have used it as their personal confessional booth. A number of faith-based organizations have jumped on the confessional bandwagon, as well.

still fairly ambiguous terms, they're a good place to start. Let's build on Surrey's ideas.

Henri Nouwen, the great spiritual writer of the last century, was a man constantly in search of connection, and his many books represented that search. He wrestled with feeling loved even as he wrote about being the beloved (*Life of the Beloved*). He wrestled with hope as he spiraled down into the inky depths of depression (*The Inner Voice of Love*). He reflected on life in the face of his own mother's death (*A Letter of Consolation*). And even though he was a Dutch Catholic priest, his largest audience, by far, was American Protestant evangelicals. The paradox of Nouwen's life and his message brought hope and healing to millions of readers around the world. His popularity revealed just how well he understood the human condition. He described it this way in his book *Lifesigns*:

> *Probably no better word summarizes the suffering of our time than the word, "homeless." It reveals one of our deepest and most painful conditions, the condition of not having a sense of belonging, of not having a place where we can feel safe, cared for, protected, and loved.*

Nouwen claimed that human suffering was the experience of "not having a place where we can feel loved, safe, cared for, and protected." He explained that this is what it means to be "homeless." We can use the inverse of Nouwen's definition of suffering to help us find a more clear definition of connection:

The kind of connection we're longing for—whether consciously or unconsciously—is the kind that creates a sense of belonging within us, a sense that we are "safe, cared for, protected, and loved." In other words, we feel most at home—most *ourselves*—around people with whom we experience that deep and authentic connection that Janet Surrey talked about. As such, we know that, whatever else connection means, it has to include the qualities that most make us feel "at home" in the world.

Finally, listen to this simple dictionary definition, one of several found for the word *connection*:

> *A friend, relative, or associate who either has or*
> *has access to influence or power.*

This is the definition we use when describing someone who got where they are in life because they had "great connections." But it's also a description of the *kind* of connection that matters. We might say, then, that the recipe for the kind of connection we're trying to define is one that includes authenticity and depth. It is sprinkled with protective safety and dignifying freedom. It contains heaping portions of loving concern for our becoming a better, more whole person. It is seasoned with access to transformative power.

When used in its very best sense, the word *home* summarizes this definition perfectly. Most of us come from homes that have been fractured in some ways. Many have not been safe, nurturing places. We haven't always gotten the support and protection we needed. But ideally home was meant to be all of those things—a safe, nurturing, transformative environment where who we are—just as we are—was always celebrated. A place where our highest potential was encouraged and sought after. When we go looking for a best friend, we go looking for home. When we go looking for a spouse, we go looking for home. When we turn our attention to the divine, to spirituality of all kinds, to God Himself, we are looking for home.

There is a truth about our longing for home—our search for community—that emerges from the beginning of the Bible in the second chapter of Genesis: "It is not good for the man to be alone." God makes this profound observation immediately after breathing His Spirit into Adam. God has just created something that appears to be incomplete; it's missing something. Has He made a mistake? What does God do in light of his conclusion that "it is not good for the man to be alone"? The answer seems to emphasize the need for a certain *quality* of connection. God's response to incomplete Adam: "I will make a helper suitable for him" (Gen. 2:18). To be clear, God was not making a statement about gender roles, assigning women the collective position of "administrative assistant."[7] Nor was He making an isolated statement about the preeminence of marriage (though marriage, with its qualities of mutual submission, self-sacrifice, and unconditional love, has always been a biblical archetype for every kind of community). Rather, God was clarifying that the

---

7 For helpful and thought-provoking resources in the study of biblical equality, visit Christians for Biblical Equality at www.cbeinternational.org.

fullness of our humanity could only be truly expressed through relationship with a suitable other.

The key word here is *suitable*. What *kind* of connection would best "suit" Adam? What quality of relationship would not only meet his basic needs for "home," but also help him grow and flourish? Badgers, despite their sassy attitude and rugged good looks, did not "suit" Adam. Could he find this quality of connection with a giraffe? Could he teach a parrot enough words to connect in conversation? Adam found himself in what was likely the most beautiful garden ever imagined—couldn't it have been enough for him simply to connect with nature? While Adam's ability to care for and relate in healthy ways to his environment was vitally important (as it is for us today), his greatest need for connection was with one of his own. The quality of connection capable of meeting Adam's need for home was to be found in intimate relationship with another human being. He needed one of his own and that's what he got—perfectly matched Eve (for whom Adam was also a suitable helper). Remember, Adam was surrounded by creatures. He lived in a world saturated with life; there seemed no end to his connections. But by intentionally creating both Adam and Eve (and every man and woman since) "in His image" and placing them in unique relationship with one another and with Himself, God demonstrated that the quality of a connection clearly matters.

Think back now to the book's introduction. When the ribbon was cut and hundreds of people began to make their way across the Millennium Bridge, their individual footsteps generated energy. At first this energy was random, firing all over the place. But very quickly the energy became "synchronized." It began taking on a life of its own as it passed through various points in the bridge's structure. That new synchrony, or new "order," forced the pedestrians to begin walking in step with one another, waddling en masse in a "skating gait." The event pointed toward the first "reality" we discovered in the case of London's Millennium Bridge. Here it is again:

1. There is a force that is capable of synchronizing a large population in very little time, thereby creating spontaneous order.

Now consider this: In the first quarter of 2009, five million people joined Facebook *every week*. In addition, Facebook's membership *doubled* from one hundred million to two hundred million people from August 2008 to March 2009. Perhaps most incredible, the vast majority of its members—140 million, in fact—have only been on the rolls since February 2007. That's 140 million *new* users in just over two years. Facebook isn't just a white-hot social-networking platform. It is a radical example of Steven Strogatz's *spontaneous order*.

In a very short period of time (five years), a very large population (several hundred million and counting) has been synchronized (pulled into the orbit of a single Web platform called Facebook). And what kind of gravity is capable of accom-plishing such a feat?

The human need for *home*.

It might sound a bit ridiculous. After all, who would claim to be looking for home in a social-networking site like Facebook? We're there to keep in touch with friends and family, to make some new friendly connections or reconnections, to share small slices of our personal worlds through pictures and status updates and playful games of Mob Wars. We just want a little mindless entertainment, for heaven's sake. But as we'll begin to see in the next few chapters, home is exactly the kind of connection that Facebook is offering. For now it is enough to say that the human need for home is plenty powerful enough to create a spontaneous order all its own. Not even Steve Strogatz saw this one coming.

But what is the nature of this new "order" and how does it help us make sense of this tendency to seek out home wherever we can find it? That's what we're going to explore next. And while we began this chapter on the warm, white sand beaches of Akumal, Mexico, I'm afraid we'll need to venture to a slightly less exotic locale to facilitate our exploration in the next one. I'm referring, of course, to the tiny community of Angola, New York.

TWO
REVOLUTION

Willis Havilland Carrier was born in Angola, New York, in 1876. He is the man credited for inventing modern air-conditioning. What's so impressive about that? You might be surprised.

The idea of being able to control the natural air's temperature and humidity was not unique to Willis Carrier. Similar ideas had popped up at least one hundred years before Carrier's invention. One early attempt was produced by a medical doctor named John Gorrie. Gorrie worked at a hospital in Apalachicola, Florida, a little town on the northern panhandle where you can still find a bridge bearing his name. Gorrie had many patients who suffered from malaria and yellow fever, illnesses often found in hot climates, both dry as well as tropical. They are terribly easy diseases to pick up—ask any American who has traveled to a developing nation about the number of yellow fever and malaria vaccines typically required just to leave the country— and Gorrie was getting more than his fair share of cases. He also knew Apalachicola's heat wasn't helping his patients one bit.

Gorrie's answer? Positioning a large fan to blow over a bucket of ice in order to cool the hospital rooms. It was a far cry from modern air-conditioning, but Gorrie deserved credit for getting the basic concept right. What better way to cool the air than by blowing it across the top of a bunch of ice?

Fifty years later the US Navy had not improved much upon Gorrie's idea when they were called in on a special assignment. President James Garfield was dying from a gunshot wound. If you've spent any part of summer in Washington, DC, you will empathize with our former president that the outrageous heat and humidity were not likely helping his condition. Even in perfectly good health, a DC July is difficult to bear. What could be done to ease Garfield's suffering? The brightest naval engineering minds came together to answer that very question.

Obviously money was not a problem. Resources were not an issue. This was the president of the United States, after all. Following a Herculean effort to resolve the issue in as little time as possible, the naval engineers proudly presented their solution: *blowing air across the top of a bunch of ice*. Of course, this was the US military, so everything was done with a bit more heft and flair. Their creation—a big box containing cloths soaked in ice water across which windblown air was circulated—succeeded in cooling Garfield's room by twenty degrees. That's pretty impressive. The only problem? To do so required that they melt through *a half million pounds* of ice in less than two months. The first large-scale attempt at altering the air temperature was not particularly ecofriendly.

Less than ten years later engineers were starting to get the hang of things. Eighteen eighty-three saw the premiere of the very first electrical power plant, thanks to an up-and-comer named Thomas Edison. It was built in New York City and made it possible for large electrically powered cooling systems to begin finding their way into service in food-storage facilities about five years later. But the relationship between heat and humidity was still not well understood, and it was humidity that seemed to be as much of a factor as air temperature. Engineers knew that cooler air preserved food longer than untreated air. But not by much. Tobacco, processed meats, vegetables—what could be done to further extend their expiration dates?

In 1906, Willis Carrier filed a patent for the first modern air-conditioning device. It was called the "Apparatus for Treating Air" and it was able to treat both air temperature as well as humidity. Carrier's little invention soon made him a very rich man and dramatically altered the social fabric of the United States (and that of the entire globe) in the process.

Carrier's first "Apparatus for Treating Air" was developed for a printing company in Brooklyn. The fluctuations in heat and humidity at the publishing plant kept altering the dimensions of its paper products. This in turn messed with the alignment of the ink-distribution equipment. Something was needed to normalize the building's environment. Enter Willis Carrier, newly equipped with a master's degree in engineering from Cornell. His solution cleared the way for reliable four-color ink printing and made the ten dollars per week he was paid worth every penny to his employer.

Carrier continued developing his original design. In 1911 he presented what he called the "Rational Psychometric Formulae" to the American Society of Mechanical Engineers. It was a method for calculating air-conditioning requirements and patterns for specific environments, and is still in use today. The formula allowed for the development of massive air-conditioning units for use in extremely large spaces. The general public got their first taste of this new technology at two separate locations. In 1924 shoppers swarmed to the J. L. Hudson Department Store in Detroit, Michigan. It was the first of its kind to offer shoppers an "air-conditioned" experience. That theme quickly spread to the Rivoli Theater in New York, which spent large sums of money advertising the "cool comfort" of its new, air-conditioned facilities. The American public began to flock to summer films more than ever.

Keep in mind that this was a time in history (not so long ago) when people only had access to locally grown food that had to be purchased on a daily basis. There were no refrigeration trucks to move California oranges to Idaho. There were no modern refrigerators to keep food fresh for days and weeks (or in the case of some college dorms, *months*) at a time. The milkman still delivered dairy products to front porches every day. Anyone who wanted a nice steak for dinner had to visit their local butcher that same day and would rarely buy anything more than what would be used for a single meal. If a family could afford ice—which was shipped in large, cumbersome blocks—it might be able to keep those same products fresh in an icebox for an additional day or two, but that was it. Everything eaten by consumers was locally grown and had a very brief shelf life. But air-conditioning changed all of that. Within two decades of its invention, just about any kind of food from just about anywhere in the country could be packed, shipped, stored, and enjoyed whenever and wherever the consumer felt like it. Daily grocery purchases (that often consisted of the basics: milk, bread, meat) turned into once-a-week shopping sprees. The result? The rise of the supermarket. Most mom-and-pop operations were eclipsed by these new mammoth grocery stores that also created the space for an endless variety of product lines to explode.

Working conditions were also impacted by the invention of air-conditioning. Manufacturing plants could now be established anywhere without fear of workers collapsing from the heat. Their construction mushroomed around the country, accompanied by an exponential increase in pharmaceuticals, textiles, meat processing, and tobacco (does anyone have a grandparent who *didn't* smoke?). Everything was becoming cheaper and more available. The economy was shifting. Unfortunately it shifted a little too much (perhaps one of the few changes that air-conditioning cannot take credit for), and the Great Depression began making a dent in the industrial forms of air-conditioning. But Carrier wasn't especially worried. He could see a trend coming that would take air-conditioning from the occasional department store to every last little home in America.

Though the first air-conditioning system for a private residence had been installed in 1914, it wasn't until after World War II that the sales of individual air-conditioning units for family homes began to climb steadily. And by steadily I mean *astronomically*. In 1948 around seventy-four thousand units were sold. By 1953—just five years later—that number had increased to well over one million units sold. Talk about *spontaneous order*. Everyone was rapidly "syncing up" to this latest development in technology. And as they did, new social changes began to emerge that coincided with the architectural advantages introduced by the invention of air-conditioning.

Until air-conditioning arrived, new home construction (especially in the American South and Northeast) was primarily concerned with how to keep the house cool during long, wretched summers. Wide eaves, deep porches, attics, thick walls, high ceilings, and a special attention to the position of the house on the property were all developed around the need to keep houses cool. With air-conditioning, virtually all of these factors became unimportant. The Victorian style (that included all the elements just listed) began to die. The "ranch house" style of architecture was born. Large pane windows, more rectangular shapes, lower ceilings, and structures that could be fit anywhere on a section of property independent of cross breezes, took the country by storm. Those noisy, drippy, metal boxes that hung outside the windows of just about every new home in America were literally changing the country's landscape.

Similar "progress" had already begun in the corporate world. High-rises became much, much higher, as cool air could now be pushed into any structure's extremities. Offices could comfortably house hundreds and even thousands of employees in one location throughout the year. Even up into the 1940s, window awnings were still used in the construction of skyscrapers to shield offices from scorching heat. But no need anymore. Glass could be used from floor to ceiling on every level. Behold the modern skyscraper with all of its shiny surfaces. City centers began to literally sparkle with their new architectural jewels.

Just when it seemed that the reach of air-conditioning had extended as far as possible, another unique trend emerged. In the early 1960s, and for the first time since the Civil War, the masses began moving south, reversing a trend toward northern relocation that had occurred in the first half of the twentieth century. If you happen to live in Phoenix, Houston, Las Vegas, Miami, or any number of other cities and towns in especially hot and/or humid parts of the country, you owe Willis Carrier a thank-you. Without air-conditioning it is unlikely such places would ever have come to be settled in such massive numbers. A map of the United States might look very different today.

But shifts in national architecture and geographic development seemed to bring with them a shift in the way people related to one another. For example, as the front porch disappeared from the average home, so did a normal rhythm of connecting with neighbors. As entertainment and social events moved indoors, the shared experience of the neighborhood began to shrink. The world was beginning to connect in ways it hadn't before, and the effects were noticeable, especially in the hot and humid American South. Raymond Arsenault, a history professor at the University of South Florida, described the change this way: "General Electric," he wrote, "has proved a more devastating invader than General Sherman."

If you can name it, air-conditioning probably had a significant impact on it. It changed the way we eat and shop. It changed the way we manufacture, advertise, and sell goods and services. It changed the way we work, where we live, how we play, what we build, and where we travel. It even changed the way we relate to one another.

Willis's "Apparatus for Treating Air": a simple little technology that revolutionized nearly every aspect of American culture as we know it.

Harvard University is known as one of the finest educational institutions in the world. Its academic traditions are as long and formidable as its famously hallowed halls. It has turned out more Nobel laureates and more future US presidents than any university of its kind. Its name is synonymous with the cream of the crop in science, literature, law, medicine, mathematics, and world leadership. It is also extremely difficult to get into. Twenty-nine thousand people applied to be part of Harvard's graduating class of 2013. Only seventeen hundred were accepted. Admission to Harvard implies that your entire academic life since kindergarten (and usually prior to kindergarten) has been aimed in one direction—graduation from Harvard University. And once you get in, you stay in. Hardly anyone drops out of Harvard—it's far too much work to get there in the first place. Besides, one would have to be just a little bit crazy and in possession of an utterly world-changing idea to even remotely consider leaving a Harvard degree unfinished.

Mark Zuckerberg was just such a person who had just such an idea.[1]

There is enough printed material documenting the meteoric rise of Facebook's founder and CEO, Mark Zuckerberg, to wallpaper the entire Facebook corporate offices in Palo Alto, California. He is nothing short of a media sensation, certainly known for his outrageous success, but also for his tender age. At nineteen he debuted what was to become the hottest Web platform since Google. At twenty-three he was worth an estimated $3 billion,[2] making him the youngest billionaire in the world, just ahead of a handful of future Saudi kings. And he had plans. Big plans. During an interview with *60 Minutes* in early 2007, Zuckerberg told Leslie Stahl quite matter-of-factly, "We're on a trajectory to be pretty universal soon if we can keep our growth going."

Not national. Not global. *Universal.* Listen to Jessi Hempel, a writer for *Fortune* magazine, describe the breadth of Zuckerberg's vision:

> *[Zuckerberg's] ultimate goal is less poetic—and perhaps more ambitious: to turn Facebook into the planet's standardized communication (and*

---

1 Another Harvard dropout with big ideas: Bill Gates.

2 In March 2009, Zuckerberg "fell off" *Forbes'* list of billionaires. But then so did a lot of people. It seems 2009's recession took a toll on everyone.

> *marketing) platform, as ubiquitous and intuitive*
> *as the telephone but far more interactive, multi-*
> *dimensional—and indispensable. Your Facebook*
> *ID quite simply will be your gateway to the digi-*
> *tal world, Zuckerberg predicts. "We think that if*
> *you can build one worldwide platform where you*
> *can just type in anyone's name, find the person*
> *you're looking for, and communicate with them,"*
> *he told a German audience in January [2009],*
> *"that's a really valuable system to be building."*

In other words, Hempel concluded, considering the future of online social networking, "Facebook will be where people live their digital lives." Facebook as "the planet's standardized communication (and marketing) platform"? That's a fairly ambitious goal. But with its seemingly unstoppable exponential growth, Zuckerberg's trajectory seemed on course to quickly become a reality.

But we're getting ahead of ourselves. Let's go back to Harvard. Or rather, let's go back to immediately after Zuckerberg informed his well-educated and well-paid psychiatrist mother and dentist father that he was dropping out of Harvard and moving to Silicon Valley to build a new high-tech start-up.

The odds against Zuckerberg becoming a success in that context were formidable. True, this was a few years *after* the initial tech bubble burst in late 2000. But the Valley was still recovering. Web 2.0 (the resurgence of money-making tech development) was under construction. There was no shortage of new tech "miners" continuing to stake out their claims, but most efforts seemed in vain. The gold rush was over, according to the experts. It would take an impressive amount of bravado, at best, or a great deal of youthful naiveté, at worst, to venture out in such unpredictable economic weather. Or, as we've already noted, it would take a world-changing idea.

Like most world-changing ideas (the wheel, air-conditioning, two-ply toilet paper), Zuckerberg's was profoundly simple: Take a university's "face book"—essentially a printed student directory with photos and contact information—and put it online. An initial prototype of Zuckerberg's creation called Facemash allowed users to rate the photos of their fellow classmates in a "hot or not" fashion.[3] There was a groundswell of student interest, but Harvard administrators were not happy about it. Zuckerberg had obtained all the photos by hacking into their database, and he soon found himself studying under academic probation. His initial effort had survived only four hours.

With the help of his roommates, Dustin Moskowitz and Chris Hughes, Zuckerberg rebuilt the Facemash platform into something a bit closer to what a few hundred million people would find familiar today. It was called, "The Facebook." Two weeks after The Facebook appeared online, more than half of Harvard's student body had joined. Word got out, and forty other schools in Boston and surrounding areas wanted in. In

---

3 More specifically, Facemash randomly paired pictures of various student-body members and asked users to rate who was the "hotter" of the two. I wonder what the cumulative therapy bill was for the "not-as-hots."

four months, forty additional school networks had been added. The Facebook was a hit. Zuckerberg had clearly struck a social nerve with university students. And the possibilities seemed endless, too good to be true. Or at least too good to be ignored. So Zuckerberg hit the road for a summer to see how his idea might fare in the legendary tech trenches of Silicon Valley.

Mark Zuckerberg grew up in affluent Dobbs Ferry, a New York suburb. He went to some of the best schools in the area. He began programming computers in the sixth grade. By the time he graduated from high school at Phillips Exeter Academy, he and Adam D'Angelo (who would become Facebook's chief technology officer) had built a plug-in for the Windows MP3 media player, Winamp. Their creation could "learn" your music preferences and build a playlist accordingly to meet your tastes. They posted it online and offered it as a free download. Companies like AOL and Microsoft immediately came knocking. "It was basically, like, 'You can come work for us, and, oh, we'll also take this thing you made,'" Zuckerberg said. He and D'Angelo declined the offers and headed off to college instead. All that is to say, Zuckerberg knew his way around computers. And when he finally moved from the East Coast to Silicon Valley after his sophomore year at Harvard, it wasn't like going away. It was like coming home.

Less than an hour south of San Francisco lies legendary Silicon Valley, the home of Google, Apple, Hewlett-Packard, Yahoo, eBay, and a sea of high-tech start-ups. It is one of the most expensive places to live in the entire world. It is the crossroads of every kind of technology and every kind of culture and ethnicity, as brilliant minds from all over the globe have been drawn like moths to the Valley's digital flame (and perhaps a hope of getting rich and making a name for themselves in the process). The surrounding area is home to four hundred billionaires and several thousand millionaires—the highest concentration of extreme wealth anywhere. The Valley is all the more appealing because it has some of the most mild winters and summers in the United States, and enjoys sunshine three hundred days a year. Interestingly it was a lack of air-conditioning—Willis Carrier's world-changing invention—that first brought people to settle the area. William Shockley, the man who co-invented the transistor, moved his research facility to the area in the early 1900s because he couldn't stand the heat and humidity at home. His move created a pipeline for other "tech" manufacturers at the time and the area soon became known as a haven for engineering minds and technological development. And of course it didn't hurt that Stanford University—famed the world over for the brilliant and innovative minds it turns out every year—lies in the *center* of the center of the Valley. Mark Zuckerberg's new home seemed perfectly suited for someone as brilliant and ambitious as himself. He promptly found an apartment, threw a mattress on the floor, and began programming as though his future depended on it.[4] Which, of course, it did.

---

4 Zuckerberg's first Palo Alto pad has often been noted—to the point of legend—for its decorative simplicity. He claimed that, at first, his furnishings consisted of a mattress on the floor, a table, and two chairs. "I cooked dinner for a girlfriend once," he told one reporter. "It didn't work well." One might blame the mind of a genius for such an empty living space—what great intellect could be bothered to decorate? Though Zuckerberg is clearly brilliant, it's more likely that his apartment simply represented the fact that he was nineteen years old, and who has a house full of furniture at nineteen?

Zuckerberg's idea was not the first on the scene when it came to building a social-networking site, of course. Not by a long shot. Friendster had been around since 2000. MySpace, founded in 2002, was the overwhelming worldwide leader, boasting tens of millions of members before The Facebook was even born. Zuckerberg was stepping onto a well-traveled path. But what set him apart from the rest was his vision. Even when investors started paying attention to what he was doing (Friendster offered him $10 million in mid-2004, Viacom and Yahoo offered him huge cash buyouts in 2006 to the tune of $750 million and $1 billion, respectively), he ignored them, much to everyone's surprise.[5]

Zuckerberg explained his maverick behavior in an interview with Ellen McGirt for FastCompany.com. "I'm here to build something for the long term," he clarified. "Anything else is a distraction." One billion dollars a distraction? Microsoft, the very same company that had come knocking just a few years earlier when Zuckerberg was a senior in high school customizing his Winamp player, came knocking again in 2007. They didn't offer a buyout this time. Instead, recognizing that Zuckerberg was on to something very, very hot, Microsoft invested enough to claim a 1.6 percent chunk of the company's value, becoming Facebook's largest business partner. Many throughout the Valley believed Microsoft made the bid in an attempt to stay a

---

5 Consider how much emotional maturity and personal confidence it would take to refuse $1 billion for your cool idea. As the offer amounts grew exponentially, so did the pressure for Zuckerberg to relinquish control of his growing empire. "Give it to someone who knows what they're doing," said many around him. "Take the money and a consulting position and enjoy your youth." Zuckerberg held steady in the face of it all.

step ahead of Google, which was drooling over Facebook and
had more than enough firepower to take it over if Zuckerberg
agreed. Either way, to market watchers, this meant Facebook
was now worth at least $15 billion. From zero dollars to $15
billion in only three years? It seemed as though money itself
was falling into spontaneous order around Zuckerberg's brilliant but simple vision.

Keep in mind, however, that while $15 billion was a formi-
dable sum, it was only an "estimated worth." What that meant
is that Facebook's future was by no means a sure thing. In 2008
it raked in only $280 million. That sounds like a lot of money,
but in truth the company didn't even break even. For all of
Zuckerberg's brilliant vision and all of Facebook's unearthly
success in adding to its membership, the company's primary
concern was still the same as every other business in a capitalist
economy—how to make money. But it's *how* Facebook began
answering that question that was not only working to secure the
company's future, but also revolutionizing the face of business
marketing as we know it.

"If there are 150 million people in a room, you should
probably go to that room," said Narinder Singh, chief product
officer for Appirio, a consulting firm that helps big companies
like Dell and Starbucks find ways to connect with consumers
via Facebook. "It's too attractive a set of people and too large a
community for businesses to ignore." In other words, it was the
consolidating effect of Facebook that was making it so revolutionary for marketers, allowing advertisers to effectively shoot
fish in a barrel. Here's *Fortune*'s Jessi Hempel again:

Imagine if an advertiser had the ability to eaves-drop on every phone conversation you've ever had. In a way, that's what all the wall posts, status updates, 25 Random Things, and picture tagging on Facebook amount to: a semipublic airing of stuff people are interested in doing, buying, and trying. Sure, you can send private messages using Facebook, and Zuckerberg eventually hopes to give you even more tools to tailor your profile so that the face you present to, say, your employer is very different from the way you look online to your college roommate. Just like in real life. But the running lists of online interactions on Facebook, known as "feeds," are what make Facebook differ-ent from other social networking sites—and they are precisely what make corporations salivate.

Facebook has two "news feeds," a personal one unique to your Facebook home page, and a corporate one, available for viewing by all of your "friends." The combination of these two feeds is what Facebook calls "the stream." When you update your status, change your info, and post pictures, videos, or stories, your personal feed gets updated. But so does the corpo-rate one. If Scotty downloads the Facebook application for his iPhone, then his stream will reflect that accordingly: "Scotty has downloaded the Facebook application for iPhone." If Lindsay becomes a "fan" of the globe-dominating band Coldplay, that, too, gets listed: "Lindsay is now a fan of Coldplay."

It did not take much imagination to see how Facebook's stream could help advertisers (whose money could then help Facebook). If they were allowed a fly-on-the-wall viewpoint to observe and track this word-of-mouth activity, they could target their audiences with pinpoint accuracy. Such would be the case if one friend wrote on another friend's wall about the benefits of Weight Watchers, for example. As soon as the words "Weight Watchers" popped up, the mega-dieting corporation could swoop in with a customized ad. "Interested in losing weight? Check out this month's special 'new members' package."

In a sense the technology was not unlike what Zuckerberg was working on back in high school with his Winamp application. Facebook was, in many ways, simply the next generation of software that could "learn" your personal preferences and customize advertisements just for you. The cumulative effect of the pinpoint advertising and unprecedented word-of-mouth access that Hempel referred to was the very thing that was making "corporations salivate."

But Facebook's revenue-generating plans were far from perfect. The main issue was, how did Facebook insert ads strategically without annoying or even alienating its members? If the strategy and its inherent problems sound familiar to you, that's because Google had been doing the very same thing for years with a great deal of success. Which makes sense because it was Sheryl Sandberg, the creator of Google's AdWords campaign, who pitched the idea when she joined Facebook as a chief operating officer. Sandberg knew that Facebook was up against some pretty daunting challenges when it came to making money in the long term. "What we have to figure out," she said in an interview in 2007, "is how do we build a monetization machine which is in keeping with what users are doing on the site?"

After all, not everyone wants custom advertisements popping up every time they mention certain products or ideas. Imagine telling your friend about the poison ivy you got during the weekend camping trip and then an ad for some new and improved "rash cream" suddenly appears on the side of your page (or worse, your *friend's* page). It might be funny or it might just as easily be humiliating (even if certain celebrities endorse said rash cream). The ability to be successful, then, will have something to do with how well Facebook advertisers can merge with the Facebook culture.

And this is where Facebook's legion of hip third-party application developers comes in. Applications, or "apps," are simply downloadable pieces of software created by third-party developers and entrepreneurs that Facebook users can then access in order to personalize their online worlds. In an interview for BusinessWeek.com, Sandberg illustrated how Facebook applications can work to increase revenue.

For example, on Valentine's Day, Honda gave a virtual gift, which was a little heart that said— I forget the exact language, but "Your heart is full, so your tank should be, too." It was a little Honda-branded gift. They paid for 750,000 of them to be given. So 750,000 people gave this

*heart to 750,000 other people. Then what that
generated on the site was talk about Honda, talk
about their cars, excitement about some of the
things they're launching, and then more than 200
million impressions. So [those ads] didn't look like
the huge ads you're used to seeing on other sites,
but what they looked like were [Facebook's] news-
feed stories. So the advertising experience itself is
very integrated into the Facebook experience.*

*There aren't that many places where an
advertiser can connect with users and do so as a
part of their experience and as part of the sharing.
We actually offer that ability.*

An entire entrepreneurial culture has sprung up around
application development on Facebook, with more than 700,000
developers generating 140 new applications every day. The culture includes everyone from young people programming out of
their bedrooms to massive corporations like Nike, Apple, and
Dell, all of whom are getting better every day at "blending in"
with their audience's environments.

But ultimately Facebook's success will really be up to its
membership. Will its members adapt to the new forms of pinpoint advertising? Will they tolerate more invasive models of
marketing? Or will they vote a collective "thumbs down" on the
whole thing and jump ship? The combined input of Facebook's
members will determine whether or not Facebook finds its stride
as a moneymaking machine in the future. And that membership

is just as curious and innovative as its revolutionary marketing power.

In 2004 a select group of very privileged university students from Boston constituted Facebook's membership. There was no such thing as Facebook without them. But that all changed in 2005, when much to its young and well-educated population's dismay, Facebook's membership roles were opened to more than just college students. Now everyone over the age of twelve could join.

The reaction was immediate and angry, but Zuckerberg and his team were undeterred.[6] The leap in membership along with its new welcoming policy piqued the curiosity of even more investors and advertisers, lending strength and credibility to Facebook, and setting it apart as more than just another flash-in-the-pan start-up. In 2007 another landmark occurred in the kind of person who found his or her way onto Facebook. That's the year that the company launched its application in thirty-five additional languages around the world. The result was yet another flood of members.

As of 2009 a whopping 70 percent of Facebook's member-ship existed outside US borders. Remember Zuckerberg's vision for a universal Web platform that centralizes everyone's online activity? The intentional move to embrace users around the

---

6 Zuckerberg has famously said, "We don't strive to be cool, we strive to be practical."

world in their own language was one of the big steps in seeing that become a reality. But an increasing variety of languages wasn't the thing that had been most shocking about Facebook's meteoric growth. Rather, it's the universal appeal to people of every age that was further setting it apart from other social-networking sites.

For example, in late 2008 the fastest-growing population on Facebook was not university students, its original target population. It was fifty-five-year-old women. That's right—your mom wants to be added as your friend. And she's not alone. Facebook's thirty-five to fifty-four-year-old demographic grew by 276 percent in 2008, and the twenty-five to thirty-four-year-old population *doubled* that same year.

As Facebook membership took on a legion of names and faces from several different generations all at once, its ability to connect family members around the globe became one of its most appealing features. What better way to stay in touch with your fresh-out-of-college son or daughter than by jumping on their favorite networking site? As more and more parents and even grandparents found their way onto Facebook's member-ship, they found something else intriguing too: old friends they hadn't talked to in years. Suddenly Facebook was becoming the ultimate class reunion. It seemed everyone was "six degrees" from everyone else. At the very least Facebook was enabling connection and reconnection in unprecedented numbers, in dozens of languages, and in hundreds of countries around the world. And that unprecedented level of connection was leading to some more remarkable numbers.

In mid-2009 eight hundred fifty million photos were being uploaded to Facebook every month, as were seven million videos. Facebook was fast becoming *the* multimedia platform on the Web, the preferred means by which tens of millions of people were sharing their lives with one another through pictures and video of travel, parties, weddings, births, you name it. As the ability to easily share media with the friends in our personal networks grew, so did the time we spent on Facebook. In March 2009, Facebookers around the world were using the site up to three *billion* minutes a day. Of course, that kind of time may be required to keep up with the 120 "friendships" that the average Facebook member maintains, to respond to the two million new event invitations listed monthly, and to accept or deny membership into the twenty-five million user groups that Facebook offers. This data brings clarity to *Fortune*'s Jessi Hempel's conclusion that "Facebook will be where people live their digital lives." In short, more and more and more people are living more and more of their lives on Facebook and, as such, Facebook is starting to take on a very familiar shape.

There is a fascinating field of science known as environmental psychology. In environmental psychology, special attention is paid to the effects of building design on human emotions. For example, studies have shown that certain colors make people feel certain things. Certain angles and materials create certain emotional responses in a person. Environmental psychology seeks to explain why this happens and to help people arrange their living spaces accordingly. Sound silly? Why pay $175 an hour so some shrink can tell you where to put your couch? Because there are certain contexts in which we humans thrive and certain others where we do not.

Raymond DeYoung, a specialist in environmental psychology, explains further.

> *People tend to seek out places where they feel competent and confident, places where they can make sense of the environment while also being engaged with it. Research has expanded the notion of preference to include coherence (a sense that things in the environment hang together) and legibility (the inference that one can explore an environment without becoming lost) as contributors to environmental comprehension. Being involved and wanting to explore an environment requires that it have complexity (containing enough variety to make it worth learning about) and mystery (the prospect of gaining more information about an environment). Preserving, restoring and creating a preferred environment is thought to increase a sense of well being and behavioral effectiveness in humans.*

DeYoung clarifies that certain environments suit us while others do not, and special attention must be paid to the things that make one "preferred" over another. In other words, not just any old environment will do and we need to understand why. In order to better understand why Facebook resonates so deeply with so many, let's look at four homelike qualities that Facebook uniquely facilitates.

1) Home is where we keep all the stuff that matters most to us.

One of the first qualities of what makes Facebook a preferred environment is its ability to contain the things that matter most to us. One of those most important "things" is, of course, our pictures. When surveyed about what three things a person might try to save if their house was on fire, the average person will almost always cite photos as their second or third choice.[7] There is something about the ability to capture, share, and preserve our life experiences in a photo (or a video) that is immensely precious to us. That is likely why those 850 million photos get downloaded onto Facebook every month. We humans have always liked to record our histories through pictures, whether they were scribbled onto cave walls or downloaded onto Facebook. Tour the average home and you'll find

---

7 When surveyed about which "one thing" we would save in case of a house fire, most people respond "family members." One clever survey-taker on Surveys.com responded, "If I could save only one thing, it would be my girlfriend holding my laptop and my dog."

exactly the same theme. Pictures of friends, family, and special events typically line walls, shelves, bedroom dressers, and table-tops throughout.

In addition to photos, home is a place that contains evidence of our values and beliefs. Many families decorate their homes with Bible verses, wisdom sayings, and inspirational thoughts. We might also display a flag or some other symbol of national or ethnic pride. On Facebook we can declare our religious beliefs as well as our political affiliations. Some do this in great detail, using the tiny space for "religious beliefs" and "political beliefs" to evangelize the masses: "Jesus is Lord and Savior of all!" "There is no God." "Republicrats rule!" Others prefer simple or mysterious statements of faith: "Christian." "Spiritual." "I believe in the trinity—me, my wife, and my daughter." "Political and religious beliefs—aren't these the same thing?"

Of course, we can also share less potentially volatile information. We can explain who our heroes and heroines are and why. We can talk about (and post pictures of) the TV shows, books, movies, and activities we like most and least. We can identify ourselves with certain groups, causes, church affiliations, and fan clubs. Do you remember how your high-school bedroom tried to reflect everything about who you were as a person—your likes, dislikes, beliefs, affiliations, and attitudes—in the space of just four walls? Facebook serves a similar end, allowing us to decorate our pages with any kind of flair necessary to demonstrate the things that are closest to our hearts.

2) Home is wherever we find family.

Just five months after World War I began, it was already becoming the bloodiest conflict in world history. Headlines from around the globe were filled with terrible news from the front. Images of endless dead bodies lying in miles of muddy trenches filled the public's imagination. But on Christmas Eve 1914, something entirely unexpected happened that created a spark in a very dark place and time.

With the day drawing to a close, both British and German soldiers defended their respective portions of no-man's-land. At that time, fighting conditions were especially miserable. Food supplies, clothing, communication devices—everything was inadequate to meet the challenges found at the front. So the soldiers from both sides found themselves standing knee-deep in icy mud, separated from friends, families, and lovers, facing a dark, cold, hungry Christmas with rifle in hand.

At some point that December 24 evening, some German soldiers reportedly managed to sneak a chocolate cake behind their British enemy's lines. The cake came with a note asking for a cease-fire to celebrate Christmas (as well as their captain's birthday). The British soldiers were shocked—and wary—but responded in kind with a gift of tobacco for their German counterparts. At seven thirty that evening, the German soldiers began singing Christmas carols. Imagine the unearthly sounds drifting across the mud as dozens of young German men sang "Stille Nacht." The British soldiers responded with heartfelt applause, then launched into some of their own carols. Soon

"Merry Christmas" was shouted across enemy lines in each other's native tongues. Finally, a few brave soldiers came out of the trenches, unarmed, and made their way to the opposing side to greet one another in person. The black-and-white pictures from that famous event are astounding. They reveal enemy soldiers embracing one another, smiling and carrying on for the camera as though it were a family reunion.

As we can see in the example of the Christmas Eve Truce of 1914, so great is the human need for home that we will re-create homelike moments wherever we happen to find ourselves, even in the middle of traumatic events, even in the experience of physical and emotional isolation. This is one of Facebook's strengths: facilitating quick and easy homelike moments with family and friends from around the world, despite any geographical barriers. It's as if we can gather all of the people closest to us under one roof and have access to them all the time.

In the real world, meeting together in this fashion would be rather difficult to pull off (and most therapists might advise against it). At the most, we might have the "everyone under one roof" experience during a holiday or a family reunion—and we all know how traumatizing that can be. But in our Facebook "homes" we can meet in an ongoing fashion and enjoy each other's company within a single controlled environment. We can easily share information and photos from our family vacations, new births, weddings, and graduations. We can chime in on current events: "I heard you guys won the game last week—nice going!" or, "Sorry to hear you didn't get that job." We can wish each other a happy birthday, a happy anniversary, a merry Christmas. Indeed, sharing memories no longer has to wait for the holidays or family newsletters. The sharing can now be instant and global, collecting the ongoing events of various family members into one space and time for all to participate in—a kind of Facebook family reunion without Aunt Edna's questionable chicken casserole.

3) Home is where we feel safe because we can control the environment.

There are now more than fifty years of psychological research showing that an individual's sense of well-being is inextricably linked to the sense of control they have over their environment. According to psychologist Dean Shapiro and his associates, "The findings strongly support the importance of *control* in physical and mental health. They also give credence to the psychological paradigm regarding control which can be summarized as follows: (a) Having active, instrumental control is positive, and (b) the more control you have (or believe you have) the better." If an individual cannot maintain a high enough sense of control, then that individual will often lose hope and become fatalistic. "I have no power," they will assume. "What happens to me just happens—there's nothing I can do to make my life better." Of course, it has also been shown that a felt sense of "too much control" can be negative. If an individual feels that everything is "up to them" or they are "all alone" in their decision-making, the effect can be overwhelming. In either case, however, the determining factor in people's sense of well-being is whether they maintain a reasonable sense of control.[8] We may have loved to display everything important to us on the walls of our high-school bedroom, but perhaps the most important part of that sacred space was the lock on the door. That lock meant that we had some power to decide who saw what and when, and that sense of power was vital to healthy psychological development. True, parents may have complained or we may have abused our door-locking privileges, but the lock gave us a choice, that choice gave us a sense of safety, and that felt sense of safety gave us the feeling of home.

Thanks to privacy controls, Facebook has provided users a significant amount of "control" over their digital world. In most cases we get to choose who sees what. We can allow certain friends to see pictures from our latest vacation while keeping nosy parents at bay. Likewise, "nosy parents" can communicate with whomever they'd like regardless of whether their children approve. At the same time, kids and parents can work together in the Facebook realm by utilizing its privacy controls; kids can connect with friends and family members freely while parents

---

8 As we saw in the last chapter, connection is the key to happiness. The fact that individuals require a certain felt sense of control does not contradict that, but only affirms it. On the one hand, if we cannot choose our connections—say, if they are forced on us by someone in authority—then we remain stuck, feeling powerless. On the other hand, if we get to choose our connections, then that sense of hopeful empowerment increases. In other words, we are happiest when we have a reasonable amount of control over the connections we make.

respectfully monitor incoming messages on their kid's page. This might not be appropriate if your child is eighteen, but it might be downright negligent if you're *not* doing it when they're twelve. Users in general get to exercise control by making public announcements (status updates, writing on "the wall") or speaking through private messages to one another. When building our list of Facebook friends, we can even "confirm" or "ignore" people we might not otherwise be able to in the real world. The level of control Facebook affords us is a large part of its homelike appeal.

4) Home is where we can "just be ourselves."

Ideally the home environment is where our unique gifts, abilities, experiences, hopes, and dreams are valued and affirmed. True, all too many of us do not (or did not) experience home that way. Nevertheless, the ability to feel at ease in our skin, to feel valued for simply being the person we are, is perhaps one of the clearest indicators that we are home.

Carl Rogers, the famous, much-revered psychologist of the last century, did much to pioneer this idea in his field. His theory of "unconditional positive regard" highlighted the importance of the "therapist-client relationship." According to Rogers' theory, the most important thing a therapist could do in order to help a client was to affirm the client's worth apart from anything they'd done or were capable of doing. In other words, affirming the client for being "just as they are" paved the way for breakthroughs in healing.

Rogers' theory is perhaps most poignantly reflected in the beauty of the biblical gospel—literally "good news"—that Jesus modeled in the way that He lived. According to Luke 15, Jesus often got in big trouble with the religious leaders of His day for eating with "tax collectors and sinners." In fact, Jesus' actions were scandalous enough to eventually get Him killed. But why were His actions so scandalous to the religious community? Because in Jesus' day—and throughout the modern Middle East today—sharing a meal was a sacramental symbol that implied *total acceptance*. When Jesus ate with the tax collectors and sinners—the very people most despised by the religious leaders—He was symbolically offering them total acceptance, apart from anything they had done or would ever hope to do. In essence He was saying, "I love you and choose you *just as you are*." What makes the gospel so compelling is the same thing that made Rogers' theory so effective: When people are accepted just as they are, a healing freedom ensues. People begin to feel at ease in their own skin. They start to feel at home in the world, and the effects can be transformative.

Now imagine getting to say whatever you'd like whenever you'd like and still be accepted for it. Imagine getting to display your favorite pictures from your very best moments in life and have others respond positively. Imagine celebrating a birthday and getting verbal birthday hugs from a hundred friends and family all over the world. What would that level of acceptance and affirmation do for you? What would it do *to* you?

We are drawn to people and places where we feel "safe, cared for, protected, and loved," as Henri Nouwen observed. Facebook provides a safe environment where users can operate "just as they are" with almost no interference from the outside. In that sense, Facebook is a Web platform that dishes out a form of "unconditional positive regard" in spades.[9]

Think back once more to the story of the Millennium Bridge. Spontaneous order emerged unexpectedly when a few hundred people began walking across the bridge's span for the first time. The emergence of that order was the first "reality" we noted in this book: *There is a force that is capable of synchronizing a large population in very little time, thereby creating spontaneous order.* In the case of the bridge, the new order was driven by simple—though unintended—physics. With Facebook we find a few hundred million people "lining up" onto a single Web platform in a relatively short amount of time, a fact that seems to affirm Steven Strogatz's theory.

But there was a second "reality" that sprang from spontaneous order. It was this: *Spontaneous order can generate outcomes*

9 Obviously there are some limits to what content users can post on Facebook. Recently a slew of new mothers were upset because they weren't allowed to post pictures of themselves breast-feeding their babies. Why they wanted to do this in the first place is anyone's guess. Either way, the images involved "nudity" and were, according to Facebook, not allowed. The women protested that "it wasn't nudity, it was natural." As it turns out, Facebook's content limits have actually drawn users to the site, many deeming it a safer and more positive environment than its cousin MySpace, which tends to be more permissive with content.

that are entirely new and unpredictable. This was not only the case in the Millennium Bridge's opening day when the outcome was merely a few hundred bewildered pedestrians locking into a "skating gait" with one another. It was also the case when Willis Carrier filed his patent for the first air conditioner. No one—not even Carrier himself—could have predicted just how widespread the impact of his little invention would be. It changed the way we did business. It changed where we lived, where we worked, and where we traveled. It changed the way we shared our lives.

Now we encounter Facebook, a new order that Clive Thompson, a contributing editor for the *New York Times Magazine* and a columnist for *Wired* magazine, calls, "The most significant intergenerational shift since rock 'n roll." What might be the "new and unpredictable outcomes" of the unprecedented connection and control that Facebook affords? If we can truly make a home for ourselves online, what does that do to our understanding of our "real" homes, our face-to-face encounters with friends and family, our notion of who we are and why we're important?

We're going to spend the next section of the book exploring those very questions. As we do, we'll discover some of the most significant "new and unpredictable outcomes" that Facebook is generating. We'll also try to understand the positive and negative effects of those outcomes. But in order to do all that, we'll have to pack our shorts and sunscreen one more time. That's because we're headed for the desert.

This spontaneous order can generate outcomes that are entirely new and unpredictable.

THREE
DISPENSATION

Located on the southeastern coast of the Arabian Peninsula, Dubai is one of those parts of the globe that is constantly generating headlines. It is a patch of white desert bordering the bright blue Persian Gulf that barely separates it from Iran. Culturally, Dubai traces its roots back to the beginning of Islam in the seventh century. But commercially, Dubai is much younger. Established as a trading center in the early nineteenth century, it did not become an official "emirate" (literally, a "prince's territory") until 1971. Since then, and especially after its reinvention following the Persian Gulf War in the early 1990s, Dubai has achieved international status as a business hub as well as a world trade center. It has also become known as home to some of the most outrageous real estate under the sun.

Dubai's Burj al Arab, for example, is the second-tallest building on the planet. It bills itself as the only "7-star" hotel in the world, and its famous sail-like silhouette is an ultraluxury destination that only the most affluent world travelers and businesspeople can afford. Many rooms contain marble staircases and personal butlers. It houses the largest indoor atrium anywhere, and one of its seven in-house restaurants rotates in a circle six hundred feet above the white-sand beaches below (the perfect place to thoughtfully sip their $35 "Burj Royale" cocktail). But the Burj al Arab is rather unimpressive when compared with the recent creation of three man-made parcels of land known collectively as The Palm Islands.

The original design for The Palm Islands was reportedly conceived by Sheikh Muhammad bin Rashid al Maktoum, the ruler of Dubai (whose family has ruled Dubai since its inception). On a napkin he sketched the shape of a palm tree and mentioned how nice it would be to build a series of islands that looked just like it. Perhaps it could increase Dubai's tourism while increasing its coastline in the process, the sheikh reasoned. Developer Nakheel Properties took it from there and within months had begun the arduous process of building an island from scratch.

To bring the sheikh's vision to life required *terra-forming*, which simply means "earth-shaping." But the definition is the only thing that's simple about terra-forming. To build an island where it has never existed previously required a great deal of sand, as you might imagine. Ninety-four million cubic meters, to be exact. And that was just for the first of the three islands;

the famous Palm Jumeirah.[1] Construction also required a relatively firm surface on which to place all that sand so that the sand does not dissolve—in biblical fashion—under any structure built on top of it. And that means you also need a lot of rock—5.5 million cubic meters' worth. But in the case of the Palm Jumeirah and its island cousins, the rock was to be built upon the sand—a time-tested design familiar to the Dutch engineers that were enlisted to assemble the pieces. Why Dutch engineers? Because the Dutch have managed to increase the coastline of their country by 35 percent. They are experts at manufacturing new earth. And luckily for the sheikh, the Persian Gulf is an ideal place to manufacture an island. It is shallow enough and narrow enough to keep out most large wave-generating storms. It's also home to a lot of sand and rock.

Island construction began on the Jumeirah by building a massive breakwater. The Palm Jumeirah's breakwater reached out of the sea by three meters (around ten feet) and wrapped its eleven-kilometer-long arms (around seven miles) around the future "palm fronds" that would give it its distinctive palm tree appearance. The breakwater, in fact, was fashioned in the same way as the rest of the island. First, sand was dumped on

---

1 The Palm Jumeirah officially opened on November 20, 2008. Its inauguration ceremony cost a reported $20 million. Celebrities from all over the world were flown in to draw the world's attention even more to the tiny desert community. A choreographed fireworks show that involved nearly every square meter of the island was the climax of the event and was designed by the same team who had put on the opening ceremonies for the 2008 Beijing Olympics. The event—like the island itself—could easily be seen from space.

the ocean floor to build up the island's base. On top of that was dumped endless rubble that further built on the sand and eventually poked through the water's surface. Finally, on top of the rubble were placed tons and tons of massive rocks.

In my mind this process seems backward. But I am neither Dutch nor an engineer. Either way, this terra-forming process was repeated constantly for three years until, lo and behold, the clear shape of a giant palm tree emerged from the sea. Once completed, the artificial palm fronds were covered with row after row of ultraluxurious homes, condos, and hotels that now stand as a testimony to human ingenuity, relentless hard work, and the power of doodling ideas on napkins. Two more islands—the Palm Jebel Ali and the Palm Deira—were well under way by the time the Jumeirah took shape (although the Palm Deira is not expected to see completion until 2015), but The Palm Islands were only the beginning. The relentless team at Nakheel Properties, the same development company that pioneered The Palm Islands, saw the potential for something even bigger on the horizon.

As though Dubai real estate were not outlandish enough, Nakheel unveiled plans in 2003 for a new development called The World. You've likely seen pictures or YouTube video capturing images of The World. The development is essentially an archipelago of three hundred man-made islands that are patterned after the Earth's own continents and countries. From a few thousand feet above the water's surface, an observer can make out the clear outlines of a "North America," an "Africa," even an "Antarctica." The entire planet's shape has been reproduced and miniaturized in sand and rock, four kilometers off the coast of Dubai.

What makes The World an even more remarkable undertaking is the fact that the individual "countries" can be purchased and developed at will by anyone with enough cash and imagination to make things interesting. In other words, Nakheel Properties may have built the planet, but individual investors get to decide exactly how they want their own little part of the planet to look. For example, a group of Irish business leaders have laid claim to the "Ireland" portion of The World and are reportedly developing it into an Irish-themed resort. In April 2008 the Salya Corporation bought "Finland" and "Brunei" with an eye on turning them into "fashion-themed" resorts.[2] By early 2008, 60 percent of the The World had already been claimed by investors interested in the custom development of their own little worlds.

In 1979's legendary and hilarious *The Hitchhiker's Guide to the Galaxy*, the late Douglas Adams imagined a particular planet whose sole purpose was to custom-build *other* planets for the fabulously wealthy. The residents of Magrathea busied themselves by constructing planets made of gold, planets made of platinum, even "soft, rubbery planets with lots of earthquakes." Whatever a person could dream up, the people of Magrathea could build. In fact the Earth, according to *Hitchhiker* lore, was built by Magratheans as a massive

---

2 What is a "fashion-themed" resort exactly? Your guess is as good as mine. "Yes, ma'am, you'll be staying in the Pegged Parachute Pants wing. It's very exclusive—Members Only, you know."

supercomputer, the purpose of which was to calculate "the ultimate question to life, the universe, and everything."[3] What is remarkable about Adams' cleverly imagined science fiction is that the creators of The World have turned it into a reality. Imagine it: getting to build a world individually suited to your exacting tastes and desires, a place where *you* decide how things work, where *you* get to choose who is "in" or "out." In such a world, you would be the ruler of your own kingdom, you'd call the shots, you'd be the center of the universe. The developers of The World islands recognized the concept's appeal from the beginning. Read the first of "seven principles" from The World's Web site describing the experience of owning and developing your own island:

> *In an era of multiplicity and me-too, it's hard to stand out. But in times like these, it's still possible to be the sun in your own universe. Welcome to your very own blank canvas in the azure waters of the Arabian Gulf. Where orchestrating your own version of paradise—whether it's a resort hotel or condominium communities—is a much-needed inoculation against the ordinary, and where*

---

3 As any fan of the *Guide* knows, the "ultimate answer to life, the universe, and everything" had already been revealed by the great computer, Deep Thought. The answer was "42," a figure Deep Thought claimed would make perfect sense once the "ultimate question" was known. Thus the Earth was built to find the ultimate question. In the end the ultimate question to "life, the universe, and everything" turned out to be—much to the chagrin of those who had been waiting ten million years to hear it—"What is six times seven?"

you'll discover that The World really does revolve around you.

"No man is an island," wrote John Donne. That may be true, but thanks to Nakheel Properties, every "man" can own one and can develop it into his or her own little version of paradise. The World's creators have turned Douglas Adams' science fiction into a reality. And investors have responded with fistfuls of cash. But why wouldn't they? After all, is there anything so appealing to our human nature as the idea of getting to own and operate our own little world?

In her essay titled "Virtual Friendship and the New Narcissism," Christine Rosen discussed the appealing nature of Facebook by likening what we find in the virtual world of Facebook profiles to the painted portraits found in the ancient world. "Self portraits can be especially instructive. By showing the artist both as he sees his true self and as he wishes to be seen, self-portraits can at once expose and obscure, clarify and distort."

As if to illustrate Rosen's "self-portrait" theory, Philip Guo, a PhD student at Stanford University, created a list of the most common pictures people use for their Facebook profiles. He mentioned the Buddy-Buddy, a photo where you are pictured with a close friend of yours. There's the Face-Cropper, a "particularly good shot of you but that also contains a friend of yours and so must be trimmed so that just you appears." Don't forget the Zoolander, wherein you pucker up "like a good male model should." Some people use cartoon versions of themselves, perhaps a Simpson-ized ideal self or a South Park rendition or simply a caricatured look-alike. Guo refers to these as Surrogates. Other users get creative with their Apple computers, contorting and twisting a picture they've snapped with their built-in laptop camera ("the Amateur Photoshopper"). There's also the Beach Bod ("hopefully looking hot"), the Musician (a photo of you playing some instrument), and the Mystery (which in the early days of Facebook meant leaving the default "question mark" in your photo's place).[4]

Whatever kind of picture we use to represent ourselves, it seems that our overall Facebook profiles do indeed serve as a kind of self-portrait. After all, Facebook allows us to arrange the elements of our page around its very simple framework, as though it were our own blank canvas. By the way we arrange our canvases, we can invite observers to notice certain aspects about

---

4 I've made some additional observations about Facebook profile pictures. For example, there are countless pictures wherein the subject is posed with an alcoholic beverage (or three) in their hand(s), smiling broadly, clearly surrounded by friends while attending some celebratory event. This might be called the "Life of the party." There are also a great many profile pictures that show parents holding their new babies. We can refer to these as "Look! I've procreated!" Or sometimes it's just a picture of the baby, sitting alone as though they were the owner of that particular page. The baby is often dressed in some adorable Baby Gap outfit and propped up against a teddy bear or a pumpkin or something equally complementary. This kind of picture is closely related to one of the strangest surrogates I've come across—the sonogram of someone's future baby. Thanks to Facebook, many of us have seen the inside of women's wombs more than we might care to. Finally, I've noticed the "I'm taken" picture. This is the sort of photograph where a Facebook user is lovingly grabbing, holding, or kissing (or all of the above) their significant other as though all of life were unicorns and lollipops. One can confirm the truth of the picture by glancing down at their Relational Status to find something along the lines of "In a relationship with ..." or "It's complicated" or "Caught up in an endless, codependent, on-again/off-again cycle with ..."

us even while we keep certain other aspects hidden. We can highlight our successes and downplay our failures. Certainly, if we do list our failures, we can spin them into some hilarious version of the real story, poking fun at ourselves as a way of de-emphasizing the blemishes (or actual pain) in our lives. We can keep taking our own picture until we get "just the right one" that captures everything we're trying to communicate in one little frame. And as we've already noted, Facebook allows us to decide who's in and who's out—who gets to see our self-portrait and who does not—by who we "confirm" or "ignore" to be in our friends list and how much we let them see via our privacy settings. "Like painters constantly retouching their work," writes Rosen, "we alter, update, and tweak our online self-portraits; but as digital objects, they are far more ephemeral than oil on canvas."

B. J. Fogg is the director of the famous Persuasive Technology Lab at Stanford University. Among other things, he has taught a class about Facebook to inquisitive parents and has coedited a book about the psychology of Facebook.[5] Fogg seems to echo Rosen's self-portrait theory when he notes that the popularity of the social-networking giant is rooted in a platform that allows users to "present yourself to the world in the way you want people to perceive you." In other words, Facebook's appeal has

---

5 As of this writing, *The Psychology of Facebook* was still awaiting publication. I'm guessing it will be an interesting read given *Fortune* magazine's nod to Fogg as one of the "10 New Gurus You Should Know," and his brilliant work at Stanford studying how computers are changing the way we think and learn. In contrast I have never been referred to as a "guru," though my mother did once call me "special for my age," which, in hindsight, may not be a compliment.

something to do with how it allows us to rule our own little world. It has something to do with *control.*

In the last chapter, we talked about four qualities of Facebook that made it feel like "home." The third quality was, *"Home is where we feel safe because we can control the environment."* When we were teenagers, having a lock on the door gave us the option of keeping certain people out, and of controlling (to a certain extent) who saw what and when. The lock, we noted, gave us a choice, that choice gave us a sense of safety, and that felt sense of safety gave us the feeling of home.

Having control means having the ability to choose. It means having options. The appeal of owning our own island has to do with the freedom to control our environment, to choose how we want our environment to look and who we allow to share our environment with us. The more choices we have, the more control we have. Conversely, when our choices are limited or nonexistent, our control is likewise limited or nonexistent.

Facebook, of course, provides us a significant amount of control in both creating and operating our own little world. In the first place, we are empowered with a seemingly endless number of choices as to how our world will look. Which pictures should I post? What should I include in my personal information? Should I add this or that application to my page? What should I say in my status update today? To poke or not to poke?

But that's just the tip of the iceberg. The biggest way Facebook gives us control is by opening to us a world of choices about whom we can add to our friends list. And when we add them, we are given more than the option of just looking at their contact information. We are also given the choice (in most cases) to see their pictures, read their stories, learn about their work lives, and review their travel histories—among many other options. Facebook even goes so far as to "suggest" friends for us; we are literally empowered and encouraged to go "friend-hunting," to simply and easily add to our collection by clicking "add to friend." And there are many more choices—reconnecting with long-lost friends, connecting informally to those with whom we'd normally have a purely professional relationship (bosses, coworkers, teachers), even starting our own groups and fan clubs.

That's a lot of choices. That's a lot of control over our social worlds. But are we better off for it?

Control is key to our sense of well-being. When we believe we have a reasonable amount of control over our lives, then we feel optimistic and hopeful. We dream. We make goals. We create plans for how to achieve those goals, all with a sense that our dreams, goals, and plans matter. Psychologist Albert Bandura called this *self-efficacy*, the "belief in one's capabilities to achieve a goal or an outcome." It is the felt sense that we have a *choice* and that our choices can improve our lives and help us find our way through difficult circumstances.

On the other hand, when we do not have a sense of control—when we feel like we have a lack of choice in our lives—our
optimism and hope quickly fade. Setting goals, let alone making plans to achieve those goals, seems pointless. Feelings of
helplessness can well up into thoughts like, *What choice do I
have?* or, *What does it matter?* Typically these thoughts lead to a
felt sense of "being stuck." If that "being stuck" feeling remains
long enough, it can lead to depression or rage-filled outbursts,
as though something deep inside us knows we were not meant
to live without choice and is protesting.

But what's fascinating is that having *too much* control (i.e.,
having too many choices) generates virtually the same outcome
as having none at all. We touched on this briefly in the last
chapter, but too much control can leave us feeling isolated—
"It's all up to me"—and overwhelmed—"I can't keep up with
everything." Roy Williams, in his delightful little book on
advertising, *Does Your Ad Dog Bite?*, explains:

> *The average American cannot say "no." This is
> why he or she is average. The temptation which
> defeats the average American is a thing called
> Overchoice, a deceiver which whispers, "You don't
> have to choose. You can have it all." Overchoice
> creates a world of too many options. One of my
> senior associates, Jim Anderson, will graphically
> illustrate Overchoice by showing you five or six
> ping-pong balls. He will ask you to catch each of
> these balls as he gently tosses them to you. Everyone*

catches the first ball easily. It is only when Jim tosses the rest of the balls together that people come up empty-handed. Instinctively attempting to catch all the balls, the average person will frantically flail the air and send ping-pong balls careening around the room. The only person that will catch a ball is that rare person who will focus on a single ball.

As Williams observes, when we have too many choices—too much control—we often lose focus and "drop the ball." Overchoice keeps us average because it prevents us from focusing for very long on any one thing. And focus is absolutely essential to doing things well, whether it's building a model boat or building a relationship.

Williams' concept of *overchoice* is similar to a term that's been around for more than a decade and one we've already used to describe what we find on Facebook: *hyperconnection*. We can think of hyperconnection as the experience of having too much control—literally, *too many choices*—in regard to our interpersonal connections. Hyperconnection is to human relationships what information overload is to our finite mental bandwidth. It's the deluge of relational connectedness that overwhelms our relational capacities. Hyperconnection makes relational focus extremely challenging because it overwhelms us with options. Who should we spend our time with? Where? In what capacity? For how long? Why? Most of us simply have too many people we are trying to Facebook, email, meet for coffee, etc., and we are not able to keep up with them in more than a cursory fashion (if at all). But, as we are about to see, there is a cost to hyperconnection.

The Millennium Bridge's second reality was that "spontaneous order can generate new and unpredictable outcomes." What kind of new and unpredictable outcomes are emerging from the advent of hyperconnection? We're going to look at two: the impact on us as individuals and the impact on our shared relationships.

Linda Stone is a writer, speaker, and business consultant who studies what she calls Continuous Partial Attention or CPA. In an article for *BusinessWeek*, she described CPA by comparing it to the popular habit of multitasking:

> *Continuous partial attention and multi-tasking are two different attention strategies, motivated by different impulses. When we multi-task, we are motivated by a desire to be more productive and more efficient. In the case of continuous partial attention, we're motivated by a desire not to miss anything. There's a kind of vigilance that is not characteristic of multi-tasking. With CPA, we feel most alive when we're connected, plugged in and in the know. Continuous partial attention is an always on, anywhere, anytime,*

*any place behavior that creates an artificial sense
of crisis. We are always in high alert.*

The desire not to miss anything is reminiscent of Roy Williams'
ping-pong ball experiment. In an effort to "catch" all the "activities or
people" we are connected to, we instinctively aim for them all. But,
as in the case of the ping-pong balls, aiming for everything means
that we typically miss everything too. Like Williams observed, in an
attempt to have it all, "the average person will frantically flail the
air and send ping-pong balls careening around the room." It's this
"flailing of the air" kind of behavior that concerns Stone.

*More and more, many of us feel the "shadow
side" of CPA—over-stimulation and lack of
fulfillment. The latest, greatest powerful technologies are now contributing to our feeling of
being increasingly powerless.*

Stone notes that our habit of continuous partial attention
is having a detrimental effect on the quality of our attention.
By trying to keep from "missing out" on anything, we become
overstimulated and unfulfilled. In addition, Stone says that all
of those choices are actually *undermining* our sense of control
and making us feel increasingly powerless. This can happen
when we begin to feel at the mercy of our technology—a knee-
jerk, out-of-control kind of experience.

Internet addiction, of course, has been a well-studied phenomenon for more than ten years. Its symptoms parallel that

of compulsive gambling and is represented by a preoccupation with and an inability to control one's Internet usage. Officially the research is still out on whether or not social networking is addictive. But it is not a great leap of the imagination to see how it could be. Certainly I've heard many people report compulsive Facebook checking or complain about being "addicted to Facebook." Either way, it seems that the more power we have—in the form of more choices—the more powerless we feel.

Stone continues:

> *Continuous partial attention and the fight or flight response associated with it sets off a cascade of stress hormones, starting with norepinephrine and its companion, cortisol. As a hormone, cortisol is a universal donor. It can attach to any receptor site. As a result, dopamine and seratonin, the hormones that help us feel calm and happy, have nowhere to go because cortisol has taken up the available spaces.*

As if things weren't bad enough, Stone says, hyperconnection is taking a toll on our bodies. The overstimulating nature of continuous partial attention leaves us perpetually "buzzing" as though we'd had too many cups of coffee.[6] This

---

6 This "buzz" may, in fact, lend credence to the potentially addictive nature of Facebook. Those suffering with Internet Addiction Disorder (yes, it has its own name) typically report turning to the Internet specifically to get that buzz and also report feeling depressed when they can't have it. It might give us pause to ask, "How would we feel if Facebook suddenly stopped working?"

is not bad in the short term. There are plenty of times when we have to rush to get something done or spend more (or more intense) time with someone to achieve a goal. Ideally the buzz-inducing activity comes to an end so we can soon return to a relaxed state. But CPA prevents this by creating a felt need for extra vigilance. We have to stay on our toes lest we miss out on something.

Stone's work on continuous partial attention paints a compelling picture about the effects of hyperconnection on our minds and bodies. But what might hyperconnection—having too much control, too many *choices*—be doing to our relationships?

In his fascinating book *The Tipping Point*, Malcolm Gladwell described the concept of "channel capacity" that comes from the field of cognitive psychology. Channel capacity is simply our brain's capacity to process information. "As human beings," wrote Gladwell, "we can only handle so much information at once. Once we pass a certain boundary, we become overwhelmed." When we have too many choices—too much control—we eventually cross a certain emotional line and become overloaded. The intellectual experience of this is called *information overload*. The relational experience of this is called relational overload or hyperconnection. "To be someone's best friend," continues Gladwell, "requires a minimum amount of time. More than that, though, it takes emotional energy. Caring about someone deeply is exhausting. At a certain point, at somewhere between 10 to 15 people, we begin to overload."

Obviously, for most of us, not everyone in our Facebook friends list is our "best friend." Our Facebook lists are usually also composed of family, coworkers, classmates, old friends from high school or college, and people we may have only a passing acquaintance with (if that). However, the idea that maintaining too many relationships can overwhelm us is true even among social circles large enough to include the variety of interpersonal connections found in most Facebook friends lists.

Gladwell illustrated this fact when he talked about the famous "Dunbar Number." Robin Dunbar is an anthropologist, and in the early 1990s he published his now famous research on how the size of our brain—specifically our neocortex— determines the size of our social group. Gladwell explained:

> *If you belong to a group of five people, you have to keep track of ten separate relationships: your relationships with the four others in your circle and the six other two-way relationships between the others. That's what it means to know everyone in the circle. You have to understand the personal dynamics of the group, juggle different personalities, keep people happy, manage the demands on your own time and attention and so on. If you belong to a group of twenty people, however, there are now 190 two-way relationships to keep track of: 19 involving yourself and 171 involving the*

rest of the group. That's a fivefold increase in the
size of the group, but a twenty-fold increase in
the amount of information processing needed to
know the other members of the group. Even a
relatively small increase in the size of a group, in
other words, creates a significant additional social
and intellectual burden.

Gladwell went on to explain that Dunbar created a formula to measure the limits of social group size by measuring the size of the neocortex against the size of the overall brain. He tested this with primates initially. Then he tested it with humans. When Dunbar's formula was applied to Homo sapiens (i.e., you and me), the number turned out to be 147.8, which normally gets rounded up to the now famous "150." Gladwell quoted Dunbar's reaction to the number. "The figure of 150," Dunbar said, "seems to represent the maximum number of individuals with whom we can have a genuinely social relationship, the kind of relationship that goes with knowing who they are and how they relate to us. Putting it another way, it's the number of people you would not feel embarrassed about joining uninvited for a drink if you happened to bump into them in a bar."[7]

The wider our social circles, Gladwell observed, the more socially and intellectually burdensome they become. According to Dunbar's research, after 150, social connections literally

---

7 It is interesting to note that—as we saw in chapter two—the average Facebook user has 120 people in their friends list, a number rapidly approaching Dunbar's theorized maximum.

become "too much of a good thing." Bill Gross is a leader in
a Hutterite community in Washington State. The Hutterites
share the same tradition as Mennonites and the Amish, and
have found the 150 number proven time and again. "When
things get larger than that," Gross said, "people become strang-
ers to one another. In smaller groups people are a lot closer.
They're knit together, which is very important if you want to be
effective and successful in community life."

Of course, Dunbar's research is now more than fifteen years
old. It took place well before Facebook was a gleam in Mark
Zuckerberg's eye. How does his theory hold up today?

In a recent article for *The Wall Street Journal,* Carl Bialik
went looking for that very answer. He quizzed Dunbar about
the effects of online social networking on his original number
of 150 as the limit to how many people we can maintain in
a social group. Dunbar admitted that sites like MySpace and
Facebook could "in principle" allow users to push past the
limit. "It's perfectly possible that the technology will increase
our memory capacity," he said. But, Bialik observed, "the [key]
question is whether those who keep ties to hundreds of people
do so to the detriment of their closest relationships—defined by
Prof. Dunbar as those formed with people you turn to when in
severe distress."

Even if our capacity to mentally process greater numbers
of relationships progresses (and I don't know about you, but
150 already sounds exhausting), the question remains: How
is our increasing hyperconnection affecting the quality of our
relationships?

Dunbar's observation seemed to echo what was discovered in a 2004 study that had the provocative title of "Social Isolation in America." The study was a duplicate of a 1984 research project that held the profoundly *un*-provocative title "General Social Survey." The 2004 study found that "the number of people saying there is no one with whom they discuss important matters [has] nearly tripled" since 1984. In other words, people have almost a third fewer "confidants" in their lives—trusted people with whom they can share their most precious thoughts and feelings in safety—than they did twenty years earlier. In 1984 the average number of confidants reported by those surveyed was 2.94. Twenty years later it had dropped to 2.08. What do the numbers mean? Somehow we've each lost .86 percent of a good friend in the last two decades. While our social connections are growing exponentially, the number of people with whom we feel safe to trust the most important parts of ourselves is clearly shrinking.

Gladwell's review of the Dunbar Number and the study of "Social Isolation in America" reveals what seems to be an increasingly common experience: the more connected we are, the more the quality of our connections suffer. But why is this? Christine Rosen ventures an answer:

> *Today's online social networks are congeries of mostly weak ties—no one who lists thousands of friends on MySpace thinks of those people in the same way as he does his flesh-and-blood acquaintances, for example. It is surely no coincidence,*

then, that the activities social networking sites
promote are precisely the ones weak ties foster, like
rumor-mongering, gossip, finding people, and
tracking the ever-shifting movements of popular
culture and fad.

Relationships require, among other things, *time*. As the number of our relationships grows, the less time we have for each one. As a result our communication events (i.e., the ways in which we relate to one another) must necessarily become more superficial. After all, we simply don't have time to keep up with each one of our many Facebook friends via long emails or shared meals or extended private face-to-face conversations. Instead we have just enough time for a quick wall posting, a shared video link, or a one-sentence status update. Facebook, of course, is ideally suited for these kinds of quick information exchanges. But what's interesting is that the *kind* of communication that Facebook best enables—short, rapid-fire bursts of information—is also having a shaping effect on our relationships.

For example, very often in the business world, a short, rapid-fire burst of information is all that is needed to communicate everything intended. "Buy." "Sell." "I need it done today." "Would you like fries with that?" But short, intense communication events like these also say something about the relationship. There is an implied power-differential, for one thing. One person is calling the shots and the other one is taking orders. There is also a formality that creates an emotional distance. After all, we don't typically speak to best friends or spouses with such "businesslike" formality. In addition, our communication style on Facebook is one-way, like a walkie-talkie. I say something and you respond (or don't). You say something and I respond (or don't). In either case, what we end up with is *communicating in order to get a reaction.* This indicates that the *way* we communicate determines the *nature* of our relationships.

Emily Nussbaum, editor-at-large for *New York Magazine,* offers an example of how this works. She says what sets apart the members of the "Facebook generation" from its predecessors is that they "assume they have an audience." Columnist Patrick Reardon, who quotes Nussbaum, takes up her thought: "They have a mental image of a large group of people interested in postings such as '25 Random Things.' Part of their identity rests on an invisible entourage that accompanies them everywhere."

The assumption that the world is always watching us, hanging on every word that comes out of our mouths, is not new. As we develop through adolescence, living for what psychologists call an "imaginary audience" is part of how we organize our inner worlds. Talking or acting out ideas in our head for our "invisible entourage" helps us sort through our beliefs about ourselves and the world around us. What *is* new is a technology that takes our naturally adolescent assumption that the world is watching, and offers us a spotlight, a microphone, and a stage as vast as cyberspace from which to act out our assumption—with our legion of friends serving as an invisible entourage.

In effect the hyperconnection of Facebook changes the nature of our relationships by turning our friends into audiences and us into performers.

"The world of online social networking is practically homogenous in one sense," writes Christine Rosen. "Its users are committed to self-exposure. The creation and conspicuous consumption of intimate details and images of one's own and others' lives is the main activity in the social-networking world. There is no room for reticence, there is only revelation."

In a world of too many choices, the emphasis is on self-expression. That's because there's too little time to do anything but communicate in order to get a reaction. Self-revelation is the currency in Facebook's social economy.

Our revelations, of course, are carefully measured. Do we post this or that interesting fact about ourselves? Do we use this or that picture from our latest vacation? Do we "confirm" or "ignore" this particular friend request? How exactly do we want our little island to look? Our actions are often based on what we think our invisible entourage might like best. Even when we assume we're doing what makes us happy (and there are times when we genuinely are), there's still part of us that's interested in keeping our entourage happy. After all, we are rewarded based on what kind of information we share, and especially, how much.

Rosen also points out that Facebook is mostly a "culture of status" and that our self-revelations are largely an effort to gain more of that status. The problem with this, of course, is that relationships rooted in status-seeking and public showcasing are composed of entirely different DNA than those rooted in qualities like emotional maturity and respectful boundaries. Listen as Rosen describes the "new taxonomy of friendship":

> *Friendship in these virtual spaces is thoroughly different from real-world friendship. In its traditional sense, friendship is a relationship which, broadly speaking, involves the sharing of mutual interests, reciprocity, trust, and the revelation of intimate details over time and within specific social (and cultural) contexts. Because friendship depends on mutual revelations that are concealed from the rest of the world, it can only flourish within the boundaries of privacy; the idea of public friendship is an oxymoron.*

Public friendships—those born and bred in a "culture of status"—may be an oxymoron, but as Rosen describes them, they *look* almost exactly like the "real thing." After all, virtual friendship, just like traditional friendship, "involves the sharing of mutual interests, reciprocity, trust, and the revelation of intimate details over time and within specific social (and cultural) contexts." But just because they look the same, are they the same?

To answer that question, we might recall that, while The World archipelago may actually look like Planet Earth, the truth is, it's just a bunch of sand.

Think back now to The World island's first "principle" as described on its Web site. Here is a summary:

> *It's hard to stand out …*

> *A much-needed inoculation against the ordinary …*

> *Welcome to your very own blank canvas …*

> *The world really does revolve around you …*

Obviously these sentiments could be just as easily applied to our Facebook profiles. Certainly, among a few hundred million other users, "it's hard to stand out." But fortunately our profiles provide us with our "very own blank canvas." They are a mostly pleasant and seemingly innocuous distraction from the normal humdrum of life. In addition, our Facebook profiles are a chance for us to develop our own private "worlds" where we are in charge. Those personal profiles are the stage and our friends are the audience.

While we can certainly use all of this control to indulge in self-portrait management and perform for an invisible entourage, the underlying desire to rule, to have control, to have *choice*, is actually very good. In fact it can even be world-changing.

There is a concept in the Christian tradition known as *dispensation,* which is the belief in a "divine ordering of management of affairs and events in the world." Another word for this is "co-creation." It is the unique idea that we human beings were created to serve in partnership with the God of the universe and with each other. It's quite a revolutionary idea, and one that finds its roots right at the beginning of the biblical narrative in Genesis.

> *So God created human beings in his own image,*
> *in the image of God he created them; male and*
> *female he created them. (Gen. 1:27)*

From the very beginning, we find Creator God pressing His own image into the clay of humanity, leaving His mark forever imprinted in our nature. But what does it mean to reflect God's image and why does it matter? There are more clues from Genesis 1. After recording that, "male and female he created them," the Bible says,

> *God blessed them and said to them, "Be fruitful*
> *and increase in number; fill the earth and subdue*

it. Rule over the fish in the sea and the birds in
the sky and over every living creature that moves
on the ground." (Gen. 1:28)

Dallas Willard, philosophy professor at USC, comments
on verse 28: "God made you similar to Him and made you
to rule over all the earth. This is a command that extends
throughout Scripture, beginning in Genesis and concluding
in eternity. This is the place you have in God's order—to be
the person He intended you to be—forever." According to
Genesis the way to most clearly reflect God's image is to "rule
over all the earth"—*with* Him. This is the first clue we have
that our longing to own and operate our own little world may
not be rooted solely in narcissism. It may in fact be part of our
image-bearing nature. The next clue also comes from Genesis,
just a few verses later.

After forming the first man (the Hebrew word for "man" is
"adam"), the Bible says that, "The LORD God took the man and
put him in the Garden of Eden to work it and take care of it"
(Gen. 2:15). Adam's God-reflecting image is revealed first and
foremost in the work and care of the garden. Likewise, inherent
in *our* image-bearing nature of God is the creative work and
care of whatever patch of ground we find ourselves placed in.
Therefore our innate desire to own and operate a little kingdom is not mere solipsism (though we have the choice to take
in that direction if we'd like to). It is in fact our God-given,
God-shared destiny. Listen, as Willard explains in his book *The*
Divine Conspiracy:

We must be sure to understand what a kingdom is. Every last one of us has a "kingdom"—or a "queendom," or a "government"—a realm that is uniquely our own, where our choice determines what happens. Here is a truth that reaches into the deepest part of what it means to be a person. Some may think it should not be so. But it is nevertheless true that we are made to "have dominion" within an appropriate domain of reality. This is the core of the likeness of the image of God in us and is the basis of the destiny for which we are formed.

You and I were made to participate in a divine ordering of management of affairs and events in the world—a dispensation. We were made to have a small piece of the world over which to have creative influence. The appeal behind owning and operating our own island—even behind creating and maintaining a Facebook profile—is a truth embedded deeply in our hearts. It is in our nature to rule and to do so in partnership with God and in partnership with others.

But this co-creation business naturally raises a few questions. For example, "How should we go about co-creating? What would co-creation mean for our Facebook experience? How do we approach our social worlds, in general, with a God-image mentality?"

When Nakheel Properties began building The World archipelago—literally remaking the world in the way they saw fit—they had to have a clear picture of what was involved in the process. They needed clarity on what kinds of materials they'd be working with and how to best use those materials to get the job done. So, too, we need a clear picture of the materials we're working with on Facebook and how we can best utilize them in the business of co-creation. But, as we're about to find, clarity is not easy to come by, especially on Facebook. And even if we finally get clarity, adjusting to the new things we see can be rather challenging.

This experience is not unlike the fascinating true story of a man named Virgil, a larger-than-life character we're driving all the way to a Kentucky farm in order to meet next.

FOUR
ILLUMINATION

Dr. Oliver Sacks is world-renown for his books describing fascinating brain disorders. A neurologist by training, one of his most famous works, *Awakenings*, was turned into an Oscar-nominated Hollywood film starring Robert De Niro and Robin Williams. Born in 1933 in London, England, Sacks grew up in a family of physicians. His home life apparently nurtured a natural affinity for medicine because eventually he landed in medical school at Oxford University, followed by residencies in San Francisco and Los Angeles. In 1965 he moved to New York to begin practicing neurology in earnest. The Big Apple seemed to warm to him, because the *New York Times* eventually dubbed him the "poet laureate of medicine." If Dr Sacks' distinguished career were defined by anything other than his significant contributions to medical science (and his haul of honorary doctorates and awards from around the world), it would be the absolutely mesmerizing nature of the cases he has published.

In his famous collection of essays called *An Anthropologist on Mars*, Dr. Sacks tells the compelling tale of a fifty-year-old man named Virgil. Virgil was born on a small Kentucky farm and had poor eyesight, even as a child. That didn't seem to stop Virgil, though. He was, his mother had said, a normal "spunky little boy" in every other way. At age three Virgil contracted three severe illnesses at once: a form of meningitis *plus* polio *plus* cat scratch fever. The combination of health issues left him paralyzed in the legs and virtually blind. Little Virgil had not traveled far on the road of life before he had run into its surprising unfairness. His health took an upswing over the next year, and he recovered use of his legs and most of his eyesight. But, according to his mother, his health crisis had left Virgil a different person, and her former spunky little boy seemed to melt into a personality marked by nonchalance and passivity.

When Virgil was six, he ran into more bad luck: Cataracts had begun developing on both eyes, his doctor informed Virgil's mother. It was obvious that he was becoming functionally blind. He would never again see his Kentucky home or the rolling green pastures that surrounded it. He would never see the creek that made its way through their property. Perhaps, most tragically, he would never again see his own mother's face. That same year, Virgil began training to read braille and use a cane at a school for the visually impaired. The passivity that had marked Virgil's childhood followed him through school, but somehow he finally graduated, and, at age twenty, left Kentucky for the great state of Oklahoma.

In Oklahoma, Virgil trained as a massage therapist and found employment with the YMCA. He was good at his job and his near-blindness seemed to enhance his tactile sensitivity. Virgil's happy clients testified to the fact the he was an excellent masseuse. The Y appreciated his hard work and offered him residency in a small house across the street that he shared with a friend and fellow Y employee. Despite his challenges and plenty of bad luck, Virgil managed to carve out a decent life for himself. He enjoyed a good job, some good friends, and listening to baseball games on the radio. He seemed happy to be on his own.

When Virgil was in his late forties, he "re-met" a woman named Amy. Virgil and Amy had actually met in 1968 at a cat show,[1] and since that time, Amy had gotten a college degree, gotten married, and gotten a divorce. In 1988, Virgil called Amy up, out of the blue. That act led to three years of sporadic phone conversations, which in turn led to them "re-meeting" in person in 1991.

But before Virgil and Amy were to be married, Amy insisted that he visit her ophthalmologist. She was of the mind that Virgil needed some help in the motivation department. Despite the successful bachelor's life he had created for himself, he still lacked enthusiasm and motivation. Perhaps there was something the doctor could do for Virgil's cataracts? And perhaps that could increase his enthusiasm

---

1 One would think that, after suffering with "cat scratch fever," one would avoid attendance at cat shows. One would be wrong.

about the upcoming wedding as well as the rest of his life? Perhaps.

Dr. Scott Hamlin examined Virgil's eyes and found that, yes, cataracts had completely covered his eyes, but there didn't seem to be evidence of retinitis pigmentosa, a hereditary disease that slowly eats away at the retinas. Virgil's retinas, Dr. Hamlin decided, might actually be fine, if those cataracts were removed. Imagine, Amy tried to persuade Virgil, that the first thing you'll see is the church, the minister, and the bride! Virgil, lackluster as usual, acquiesced.

Amy kept a journal and on the day after Virgil's operation wrote:

> *Virgil can SEE! ... Entire office in tears, first time Virgil has sight for forty years.... Virgil's family so excited, crying, can't believe it! Miracle of sight restored incredible!*

What happened next was the catalyst for Dr. Sacks' entry into Virgil's life, as well as the beginning of a shocking series of discoveries about that amazing lump of cells we call the brain.

The first thing Sacks noticed when he met Virgil at an airport five weeks after the cataract operation was his size. Poor Virgil was just plain fat. "He moved slowly and tended to cough and puff with slightest exertion," writes Sacks. "He was not, it was evident, an entirely well man." Virgil's eyes darted around in his head like goldfish in a bowl, still acclimating to sight. On the long drive home from the airport, Sacks observed Virgil's inability to focus on human faces and his preference for color and moving objects. "He especially liked the bright yellow school buses," noted Sacks. At one point a speeding car passed them from behind, much to Virgil's delight. When they finally arrived at Virgil and Amy's house, Dr. Sacks described what he saw this way:

> Virgil, caneless, walked by himself up the path to the front door, pulled out his key, grasped the doorknob, unlocked the door, and opened it. This was impressive—he could never have done it at first, he said, and it was something he had been practicing since the day after surgery. It was his showpiece. But he said that in general he found walking "scary" and "confusing" without touch, without his cane, with his uncertain, unstable judgment of space and distance. Sometimes surfaces or objects would seem to loom, to be on top of him, when they were still quite a distance away; sometimes he would get confused by his own shadow (the whole concept of shadows, of objects blocking light, was puzzling to him).

Adjusting to life in a sighted world when one has been blind for forty years does not come naturally. Or easily. According to

Sacks, we learn to "see" when we connect the tactile parts of our brains with the visual parts. We come to know an object by the way it feels as well as the way it looks.

At one point Dr. Sacks pulled a blood-pressure cuff from his medical bag. Virgil couldn't understand for the life of him what he was seeing. "But he recognized it immediately when I allowed him to touch it."

Sacks described how we learn to judge distances by our ability to move through space and then connect that movement to what we're seeing, noting changes in perspective, changes in lighting and shadow, differences in the way objects are aligned with one another. Sacks noted that, in Virgil's first week of sight, he had to navigate a particular "line" through his house in order to know where he was. Thus Virgil learned that a "whiteness to the right" as he entered his house was in fact the dining table in the next room, although neither dining room nor table were clear visual concepts for him. When we do not have visual information at our disposal, the brain often compensates, redirecting the processing power allocated for visual information toward other parts of the brain. This is why many visually impaired people have a stronger sense of hearing than sighted folks. Virgil couldn't see, but he could read with his fingertips, an operation made possible by the brain's reallocation of the visual parts of his brain.

But what happens if the visual parts of the brain that have been closed for business are suddenly needed once again? How does the brain process all of that new information? We would naturally expect that restoring one's eyesight after a long blindness (or after never having seen at all) would simply allow the once-blind to clearly see once more.[2] But as it turns out, this is not what happens at all.

It's hard to imagine a world before Facebook. Even though it's only been around since 2004, it has become a staple of our social diet in both the real and virtual worlds. While there had been plenty of social networks prior to the meteoric rise of Facebook, none seemed to tap in to such a large and diverse population. This consolidating effect shifted the kind of access we had to one another's personal worlds (pictures, personal histories, friends), making it easier than ever to experience a level of "knowing" about one another, even within a very large group of people.

In that sense, we "saw" things differently before Facebook. Our social worlds prior to Facebook were more clearly divided. For example, maybe we thought of our coworkers and class-mates being over *there* and our closest friends and family over *here*. There may have been some blending of social connections, but for the most part we had more access to the personal lives of friends than we did to many of our coworkers, and that level of access is what defined the relationship.

But since the advent of Facebook, there's a new way of see-ing, one that is much broader in scope, a view that takes in

---

2 Sacks notes Mark's description of the healing of the blind man at Bethsaida as an example. "For here at first," he writes, "the blind man saw 'men as trees, walking,' and only subsequently was his eyesight fully restored."

hundreds of different relationships in one glance, all with significantly increased levels of self-revelation. Now it's less likely that
some of our relationships are *here* and others over *there*. Thanks
to Facebook, they're all right in front of us, available to us at any
moment. But this way of seeing is so new, we're still getting used
to it in many ways. Like Virgil, our "eyes" are still adjusting to the
view.

Sacks writes, "When Virgil opened his eyes, after being blind
for forty-five years, there were no visual memories to support
a perception; there was no world of experience and meaning
awaiting him. He saw, but what he saw had no coherence."

Virgil's experience was virtually identical to the two dozen
or so cases like his that have been reported throughout history.
The "seeing" world, it turns out, is one of overwhelming chaos
to a formerly blind person. This was certainly true for Virgil. He
could not focus his eyes. He could not judge distances. Walking
proved terrifying and objects seemed to jump out at him. He
would get confused by his own shadow. "Virgil's sight might be
largely restored," observed Sacks, "but using his eyes, looking, it
was clear, was far from natural to him; he still had many of the
habits, the behaviors of a blind man."

Like Virgil, when we move from an old way of seeing to a
new way of seeing, things are blurry at first. It might even be
frightening. And one of the new and unpredictable outcomes
of the spontaneous order found in Facebook is the blurring
of our social world. In many ways our eyes are still adjusting
to the reality of Facebook. We're just beginning to learn how to
navigate the new relational opportunities and styles found in

a hyperconnected context. Such unprecedented access to the personal lives of our vast and varied social network takes time to get used to, of course, and for many of us, we're still operating out of an old way of "seeing" things. Like Virgil, we've grown accustomed to a certain way of relating to the world and now have to adjust.

In her two-and-a-half-year study of the effects of social networking on teenagers, Danah Boyd observed the blurring nature of hyperconnection. She references *In Search of Place* by Joshua Meyrowitz[3] to illustrate this and notes how it applies to everyone, adults as well as teens.

> *[Meyrowitz] focuses on the ways in which electronic media collapses spatial boundaries and social contexts, blurring social roles and bringing audiences together who might not normally be co-present. Because of electronic media, information and social acts lose their context and new identities, behaviors, roles, and social situations must be formed to account for the way that social structure is changed. This, in turn, disrupts pubic and private distinctions, boundaries between social groups, and the very essence of public life. What [Meyrowitz] demonstrates with television and*

---

3 Meyrowitz wrote about the television's influence on culture, a subject that was as layered and confusing for people back then as the Internet and social networking are for us today.

other early forms of media has only intensified
since the rise of the Internet.

Boyd says our technology "collapses spatial boundaries and social contexts, blurring social roles and bringing audiences together who might not normally be co-present." This is certainly what we find on Facebook—a sometimes-confusing blend of private and public life all in one space that can make things blurry for us. As such, adjustments must be made to accommodate our new and increasing hyperconnectivity. That's why, according to Boyd, "new identities, behaviors, roles, and social situations" become necessary in order to "account for the way social structure is changed." In other words, we have to learn how to "see" in a new way if we want to move beyond the blur.

To do that, we're going to look at three types of boundaries that seem to get especially fuzzy in regard to Facebook: (1) privacy and authority, (2) peer and romantic relationships, and (3) time management and personal identity.

1. Privacy and Authority

In early 2009, Brian Dawkins, a star safety for the Philadelphia Eagles, signed on to join the Denver Broncos in his free agency. Like many Eagles fans, Dan Leone was unhappy about Dawkins' move. Also like many Eagles fans, Dan used his Facebook account to vent, going so far as to accent his feelings with an expletive. But unlike most Eagles fans, Leone happened to be an employee at the Eagles' stadium, and his boss happened to be one of Leone's Facebook friends. Leone's status update was forwarded (by his boss/friend) to the Eagles' guest services manager who called Leone two days later and fired him over the phone.

A writer for the *Philadelphia Inquirer*, John Gonzalez, interviewed Leone, who clearly stated his regret. "I shouldn't have put it up there," Leone said. "I was ticked off, and I let my emotions go, but I didn't offend any one person or target a specific individual. I was just upset that we lost such a great guy. Dawkins was one of my favorite players. I made a mistake."

Losing one's temper at a boss or venting frustration about a job is certainly human. Who among us hasn't felt anger or hurt feelings at some point in our working lives? It is likely that many of us, like Leone, have even expressed our feelings with a short and sweet status update. But when your boss happens to be in your Facebook "friend" list, the relationship gets a little blurry. It might even get you fired.

There was a time in the not-so-recent past that lines between employers and employees were fairly clear. Spending time together in a work setting was fine. Sharing limited personal information between employees and their employers (and vice versa) in order to create a friendlier work environment was also not unusual. But Facebook is changing all of that, and in Danah Boyd's words, "blurring social roles and bringing audiences together who might not normally be co-present."

But this isn't true just for the workplace; it's also true in the classroom.

Just six weeks after he joined Facebook, Rich Hall, a fifty-two-year-old theater manager from Illinois, had accumulated more than four hundred "friends," including a number of acquaintances from around town, old high-school buddies, and his car mechanic. In order to more easily coordinate rehearsals, Hall said, he decided to add the sixty high-school students he was directing in a school play. Many of the students confirmed his friend request while a few ignored it. A number of parents were concerned and felt that Hall's act of "friending" his theater students was "a little creepy." But the twist in the story came when some of Hall's new connections eventually linked him to pictures of his own nineteen-year-old son, chugging a can of beer at a Friday-night bonfire.

"He denied it and said it wasn't there," Hall said. "I said, 'Let's go to this page together and look at these photos.' Of course he did it. There are no secrets anymore."

In an article for the *Sydney Morning Herald*, Lori Aratani interviewed Lily Goldberg, seventeen, a high-school junior from Maryland. Lily said, "Having parents on Facebook just seems weird. It's like having them walk into my room." Aratani also mentioned the crisis Matt Florian, another high-school junior, faced when he opened his Facebook page only to find a "friend request" from his dad. "What are the social implications for 'friending' your folks?" he wondered out loud.

Brad Stone, the *New York Times* writer who reported the story of Rich Hall, said, "People … sometimes like to keep secrets and maintain separate social realms—or at least a modicum of their privacy. Facebook … is a force that reinvents and tears at such boundaries. Teachers are yoked together with students, parents with their children, employers with their employees."

Facebook is indeed reinventing and tearing at traditional boundaries, stirring up a hornet's nest of new issues related to privacy as employers befriend employees, teachers "add" students, and parents friend-request their children. Certainly privacy controls are available via Facebook to limit "who" has access to "what." But the problem is, these types of controls are often more illusory than real. Why? Because of the nature of cyberspace that Facebook orbits within and because of our own online habits.

The Information and Privacy Commissioner of Ontario, Canada, has published a handy little guide about online privacy that stresses the point. The guide's introduction says, "It's crucial to remember that anything posted online may stay there forever, in some form or another."

One of the most interesting things about cyberspace is that it doesn't "forget." If you've downloaded it, posted it, searched for it, or looked at it, there is probably a record of the event floating "out there" somewhere. And it is likely someone else can find that info, privacy settings or no. "Anything associated with you—or the people you're connected to," says the guide, "can and most likely will be viewed and evaluated by other people, some of whom may have considerable influence over your life, now or in the future." This was true for Dan Leone who lost his job with the Eagles. This was true for Rich Hall and his son, who became curiously tangled because of their Facebook behavior (and in the case of Hall's son, his *friend's* behavior). These kinds of events are happening more and more often and are one of the great challenges of living in a hyperconnected context.

That's not to say we're powerless against it or that we shouldn't use privacy settings whenever possible. Of course we should. Our Facebooking and Internet usage, in general, should always have a measure of vigilance. The problem is we think we can do whatever we want online as long as our privacy settings are working right, and this is simply not the case. After all, it's our own little world, right?

"What you might see as fun and meaningless in a 'wall' post or photo," says the guide, "could be interpreted as evidence of recklessness and lack of judgment by someone who doesn't understand the context. Your activities, comments and views, even though you may have just been joking around with your friends, all become part of an online resume that, inadvertently or not, becomes available to everyone."

The blurring of traditional boundaries between employers and employees, between students and teachers, and between parents and children all highlight the emerging challenge of online privacy and the way our online behavior is always public in nature. It also means that, just like Virgil, we're going to have to learn new ways of operating in such a different-looking world.

2. Peer and Romantic Relationships

As we saw in the last chapter, the nature of our online relationships is determined by the way we communicate with one
another. When we perpetually communicate via short, rapid-
fire bursts of information, we inevitably turn our friends into
audiences and ourselves into performers. But there is another
level of confusion in regard to friendship; namely, who should
I be friends with and how do I go about choosing? Andrew
Wallenstein, in an essay for NPR's *Day to Day* program, related
his own experience of wading through the muddy waters of
online friendship by telling the humorous true story of his
Facebook encounter with "Bob."

After joining Facebook, Wallenstein—like most of us—
busied himself with finding and adding friends. One day he
was surprised to find a friend request from a man named "Bob,"
an event Wallenstein found "remarkable" because he had never
met Bob. Wallenstein noticed that he and Bob did share a
few mutual Facebook friends, but decided that since he and
Bob had never met in real life, he would "ignore" Bob's friend
request. Bob—whoever he was—was not so easily deterred.
Wallenstein received *five more* friend requests from Bob as the
days went on, rejecting each one in turn. Wallenstein tried to
find out more about this so-called Bob, but the mysterious man
didn't even have a profile picture. "I started to imagine him as
Robert De Niro in *Cape Fear*." A few months later Wallenstein
had a real-world run-in with an acquaintance of his, someone that was also one of his Facebook friends. Wallenstein's

acquaintance happened to share a mutual Facebook friend. You guessed it: *Bob.* He couldn't believe his ears when his acquaintance said, "Bob thinks you're stuck up." Wallenstein was dumbfounded. "Keep in mind," he lamented, "that I had *never met this man.* Therein lies my confusion as to just what being a friend on Facebook really means." Technically speaking, Wallenstein said, Facebook friendship is simply the process of clicking "add as friend." It's the creation of a virtual connection that "really isn't too demanding of a relationship." But then, he observes, "all it entitles you to is *full access* to each other's profile pages." Originally Wallenstein joined Facebook because he thought it would be a more efficient way of keeping in touch with actual friends. "That's friends as in, 'I know you very well, I like you, I care about you.'" But after a while he wasn't so sure about his understanding of online relationships. "Little did I know that friendship meant something different on Facebook," he said. Rather, he found Facebook friend lists to be zoolike collections of "basically every human being you have ever known."

After discovering yet another friend request from Bob, Wallenstein decided that Bob, and people like him, were "a breed of Facebookers on some kind of maniacal pursuit to tally as high a friend total as possible, as though the site were offering prizes for top scores." He clicked "ignore" one more time and confessed that the cloudy waters of Facebook friendship have not been easy for him to navigate. "I've wasted so much time agonizing over the friendship-worthiness of long-forgotten co-workers or ancient ex-girlfriends that … I've contemplated

Facebook suicide," that is, the idea of removing his Facebook page altogether. "Luckily, I am just narcissistic enough to hang in there—you see, I can't bear the thought of the Internet without me."

Wallenstein's "Bob" story illustrates just how fuzzy things can get in regard to our online friendships. After all, as we've already seen, most of our online connections have the same title: "friend." Knowing who to "confirm" or "ignore" can become a source of anxiety. In addition, knowing what or what not to post is not always clear—will something we share about *this* friend hurt *that* friend's feelings? Of course, this can get decidedly more complicated when our Facebook friendships take a romantic turn.

Rarely is the "blurry" nature of Facebook friendship demonstrated so clearly the way it is in Facebook romances. Who among us hasn't stood witness to or been actively involved in the kind of relationships that Facebook narrates with sound bites like, "It's complicated," or, "Scotty is now in a relationship," "Jeff and Kelly are now married"[4] or, "Barbie is now single" (accompanied, of course, by a little "broken heart" symbol). Since we're all friends, we all enjoy a front seat to watch how our friends' relationships play out. The public nature of online romance can make things even trickier than they already are in real life.

---

4 If the couple has been married a while before the individual updates their relationship status on Facebook, this usually serves as a catalyst for a half-dozen emails from friends saying things like, "It's about time!" or, "Nice to hear you guys aren't living in sin anymore!" Such comments are almost universally followed with a happy face :-).

One humorous depiction of a Facebook fling that circulated among folks in 2008 was found on the *Chicago Tribune's* comedy Web site, Head Candy. It was titled "A Modern Day Romance" and was simply the snapshot of a Facebook news feed or "stream." The first panel read: "Kevin and Jennifer are in a relationship." Next, "Jennifer wrote on Kevin's Wall: 'Hey BOO! I wuv you, my wuvy dovy!!! ;-)'" Overwhelmed with passion, Kevin dedicated a song to Jennifer—Mariah Carey's "Always Be My Baby." Jennifer responded with a flirtatious Ninja Kick: "HI-YAHHHH!!! ;-)" A short while later, we found that "Amy friended Kevin." After pictures show up on Kevin's Facebook profile showing him at Amy's birthday party, Jennifer wrote on Kevin's wall, "Who the [heck]⁵ is Amy?" In the next panel Kevin sent Jennifer a "piece of flair" that looked like a flower and had the inscription, "Whoa, whoa, it's not what you think honey." Before long, "Jennifer joined the group 1,000,000 Strong Against That Conniving Witch Amy." Soon a post appeared that read, "Kevin has changed his number and address" followed by a final one that stated plainly, "Kevin is now listed as 'single.'"

The brilliance of "A Modern Day Romance" is that it hits so close to home. I've personally witnessed the get-togethers and breakups of numerous Facebook friends, all captured in heartbreaking detail on my Facebook stream. Worse still are the married people I've seen document their crumbling union and eventual divorce for all their Facebook friends to see. I can't

---

5 Expletive changed, as you probably guessed.

help but wonder at all the hurt behind an update that reads, "So-and-so is no longer married." The public nature of online friendship is clearly making things blurry for many who are trying to genuinely discover and cultivate authentic romance in a hyperconnected world.

But despite much of the confusion around Facebook friendship and romance, certain key themes remain consistent, at least in definition. In an online survey of three hundred adults, ages eighteen to sixty, many of whom lived in and around Silicon Valley, their emailed responses to "What is a friend?" provided some clues as to how the hyperconnected think of friendship in spite of the burring boundaries.

Fiona said, "Friends are the people who tell you that you're nuts for deciding to paint your own mural in your apartment, but come over to help you anyway. They are the people who know your strengths and weaknesses, and love you anyway."

Hardwin wrote, "A friend is someone for whom time is irrelevant. With whom truths are shared and protected. Who gives hugs with tears. Who knows how to give gentle corrections. One who gives you uplifting affirmation and encouragement. One of your best sounding boards—your Life GPS. Forgiveness personified. Your bank for shared memories, no FDIC needed."

Delia added, "A friend does not intentionally hold you from the truth (even if the truth may hurt), regardless of the pain it may cause them. Of course we are never perfect in our ability to give to others in these ways, but this definition has been a helpful roadmap."

A few others chimed in with their frustration at how the definition of friendship seems to be shifting thanks to online social networking. Daniel from England wrote, "Friends—they used to be people with whom you could trust anything, expect everything, resent nothing and love in a way that lets you know that God is up there. And then they made Facebook. Now a friend is someone you meet once or not at all, but you 'add' them anyway so you look like you've got more friends than you really do. I mean, who wants to be one of those *losers* with so few friends? Of course, I'm writing this while sitting in my bedroom all alone."

Dohee takes a different approach. "I hate this *What is a friend?* question. Not only that, but I notice a pattern of response when this kind of question is asked. It's never about what we can do for our friends, but rather what our friends can do for us. Rather than defining what a friend should be to us, why can't we start *refining* ourselves into the friends we can be for other people? Perhaps knowing what high standards people have for what they expect in a friend is what keeps us from being good friends to each other."

Wes echoed some of Dohee's sentiments and nicely summarized what many of us have experienced while trying to make sense of the blurry nature of friendship in a hyperconnected world: "What is a friend? … wow … this question holds some deep joy and some deep sorrow for me."

The writer of Proverbs said that, "One who has unreliable friends soon comes to ruin, but there is a friend who sticks closer than a brother" (18:24) and affirmed the idea that, "A friend loves at all times, and a brother is born for a time of adversity" (17:17). The human heart knows the definition of true friendship and has for millennia. At the deepest center of our being, we long for friends that "stick closer than a brother [or sister]" and recognize that, in its purest form, friendship holds a safe space for us to experience "love at all times." We have a strong intuitive sense about what a friend looks like. And yet friendship—at least in the way it's defined above—does not seem to come easily. Why?

While our hearts are clear (and the expressed *definitions* of friendship are clear), our minds can get easily cloudy about the matter. They can be ever-changing around the idea of friendship, flexing and twisting to suit our desires in the moment, causing us to relate to one another in ways that are not particularly friendlike, even when we're listed among each other's friend lists. Such dissonance around the definition of friendship further blurs the relational landscape of Facebook.

3. Time Management and Personal Identity

There is at least one more way in which hyperconnection—especially on Facebook—is making it difficult to see things clearly, and that's in regard to the concept of time management and the self. In fact, as we are about to see, the way we use our time has significant influence on the way we see ourselves.

Sherry Turkle is the founder and director of MIT's Initiative on Technology and Self in Massachusetts. In a chapter she published for the *Handbook of Mobile Communication Technologies*,[6] Turkle addressed the emerging idea of the "tethered self." The tethered self, says Turkle, is a relatively new phenomenon, the result of a collision between social networks like Facebook and mobile technology (iPhones, BlackBerrys, etc.) that is actually changing the way we think about ourselves. Turkle explains further:

> *For the most part, our everyday language for talking about technology's effects assumes a life both on and off the screen; it assumes the existence of separate worlds, plugged and unplugged. But some of today's locutions suggest a new placement of the subject, such as when we say, "I'll be on my cell," by which we mean, "You can reach me, my cell will be on, and I am wired into social existence through it." On my cell, online, on the Web, on instant messaging—these phrases suggest a tethered self. We are tethered to our "always-on/always-on-us" communication [technology] and the people and things we reach through them.*

---

6 Turkle's contribution to the *Handbook*, called "Always-On/Always-On-Us: The Tethered Self," is an excellent resource for parents who want to better understand the relationship between technology and adolescent development.

In 2007, Facebook released its application for download on both the iPhone and BlackBerry. By January 2009 twenty million people had downloaded the mobile Facebook application. This represented a shift in mobile communications. Not long ago, in the dark ages of digital technology, cell phones were used for calling people. Now we use them to play music, plan events, check and respond to emails, text until our thumbs bleed, help us find the nearest takeout pizza, and check our investment portfolio (I just checked—I still don't have one). With the creation of the downloadable, portable Facebook application, we are now able to carry with us access to each other's personal lives as well as a means through which to share our own, moment by moment. We became high-tech turtles with mobile technology for a shell; we can now take "home" with us wherever we go. Of course, what's currently unique to the iPhone and BlackBerry platforms will soon be commonplace. It won't be long before even very basic cell phones have the Web-accessing, personal world-consolidating features of an iPhone, and that emerging reality will only increase the always-on, always-on-us trend.

But mobile technology is hardly needed to tether us to our personal networks. There are tens of millions of us who check Facebook several times a day (or more accurately, several times an hour) while at work, at home, on vacation, at church. Moving quickly into the second decade of a new millennium, we are *all* moving toward a more tethered state. And perhaps more than any other single factor, our heightened ability to be always-on is changing the way we think of and define ourselves in both the virtual and real worlds. Let's look at two ways that being always-on is blurring our sense of self.

First, being always-on reinforces the belief that an invisible entourage follows us wherever we go. Our nonstop connectivity ensures we are always within reach of *someone*, at least technically, and at least in a way that might cause us to act differently than we would if we knew no one was watching. For example, our status updates are like personal headlines that we post to let others know what we are thinking, feeling, and doing. "Jack is about to go on a date with Diane." If we thought no one would ever read them, would we be so eager and so unfailing in our status updating? Or to put a twist on an age-old question, "If you update your status in the woods and no one's around to hear it, does it make a sound?"

As we saw in the last chapter, our status updating (and the growing popularity of microblogging that has turned Twitter into such a white-hot phenomenon) is fueled by the notion that we live for an invisible entourage. After getting fired from his job with the Philadelphia Eagles, Dan Leone admitted that he shouldn't have updated his status the way he did. "I was just upset," he said, "and I let my feelings go." Of course, the fact that he "shouldn't have" meant his actions had consequences. Someone really *was* watching. Indeed, every one of us on Facebook is being "watched" (at least potentially) by someone else. In many ways, that's part of the Web site's appeal. It's also part of its influence on the blurring "self," because the more we believe we have an audience, the more likely our behavior will reflect that belief. We will live in response to a thousand imagined voices, rather than in response to our own hearts.

The whole effect can undermine our self-confidence and self-concept. Turkle again:

> *[Hyperconnectivity] gives us the potential to communicate whenever we have a feeling, enabling a new coupling of "I have a feeling/Get me a friend." This formulation has the emotional corollary, "I want to have a feeling/Get me a friend." In either case, what is not being cultivated is the ability to be alone, to reflect on and contain one's emotions. The anxiety that [people] report when they are without their cell phones or their link to the Internet may not speak so much to missing the easy sociability with others but of missing the self that is constituted in these relationships.*

The cultivation of a healthy self-concept is being subtly undermined by the tendency toward always-on behavior. By way of example, Turkle mentions the fact that many kids are getting cell phones at a younger age, a reality that is having an impact on their development. The new phone is enabling parents and children to be in touch with one another, but it can prevent the child from having to face certain difficult tasks on their own. "With the on-tap parent," Turkle observes, "tethered children think differently about their own responsibilities and capacities. These remain potential, not proven." Likewise, when a young person jumps on Facebook as soon as they cross the minimum age of twelve, they are newly connected to a vast and growing network of "others" from whom they can receive guidance, comfort, and camaraderie. While this is often a positive experience—teens need access to a widening circle of voices in order to make sense of themselves and their world—it can also be potentially harmful. Young people can come to so fully depend on the advice and opinions of others— including parents—that they become stunted in their ability to navigate life on their own.[7]

Of course, this is no less true for adults. For example, many adult users will seek input from others via their status update, effectively instigating their own personal online poll. Two that popped up in my Facebook stream in the last twenty-four hours: "I'm thinking of becoming a brunette. Any thoughts?" and "I really want to get a new motorcycle—what do you guys think of this one? [Craigslist link included]" Of course, most of us don't poll our online networks before making decisions. The questions posed by my two Facebook friends were simply practical ways of participating in social-networking culture. But their informal poll-taking does represent the *internal* poll-taking we all tend to engage in when making choices on Facebook. *Should I post that picture? I wonder what so-and-so would think if I did. Maybe I shouldn't.* We silently guess at our friends' opinions, hoping to make a choice that the majority would approve of.

---

7 Obviously this represents a continuum. A thirteen-year-old will need more parental supervision than a nineteen-year-old.

This can be a positive thing. In his fascinating book, *The Wisdom of Crowds*, James Surowiecki makes a strong case for the benefits of access to a large decision-informing audience. Surowiecki argues that individuals tend to make better decisions when informed by a crowd than when they make decisions in isolation, even when they are experts on the matter. Our network of Facebook friends makes for a natural crowd that is easily accessed for use in weighing decisions, and their input may often prove helpful. But, Turkle observes, an ongoing pattern of polling for opinions "invites [us] to greater dependency." Like a habit-forming medication, we come to rely on more and more of the stuff to get back to "normal." We come to require more, not less, input from others in order to feel like we're living as we should. This results in an erosion of self-confidence and a blurring of self-concept. What do we do if we *don't* have access to the input of our online legions?

The "voices" of our invisible entourage can drown out the sound of our own hearts. We can find it increasingly difficult to know whether our thoughts, actions, and feelings are our own, or whether they are simply the collective "voice" of our large personal networks. After all, the collective "voice" is so much louder than our own. But what people expect of us and who we *really are* can often be two different things, and it is increasingly difficult to discern between them as our friends list grows and the "voice" gets louder. As a result what's been true for Hollywood celebrities is becoming true for each one of us. We, like celebrities, are faced with the tempting idea that it is better to be liked than to be ourselves. But becoming our authentic self requires that we eventually learn to stand on our own two feet, to occasionally make unpopular decisions, and to forge new paths often *despite* public opinion. Constant polling and trolling for approval can prevent this, creating a distorted image in place of a clear, authentic self.

A second way that a clear picture of "self" gets blurry is related to the way our always-on tendencies prevent us from being fully present in the moment. In many ways, we are ever-connected to anywhere other than *here* and *now*. I recently ran into an old friend I hadn't seen in many months. We had worked together for a time and overcome some difficult challenges together, so I was glad to spot him one night from across a parking lot. I called out to him, "Jeff!" Jeff turned and smiled in recognition. He ran over to greet me. But ten steps from where I was standing, he stopped dead in his tracks. He looked down, reached into his pocket, and, right in front of me, silently checked the email on his BlackBerry for about thirty seconds. I was shocked. He explained a moment later that he was "waiting to hear back on a particular project." I lied and said, "I understand." The truth was, I felt foolish, wrongly assuming that I had meant more to him than the impending arrival of his next email. In hindsight, however, I can't blame him. Being always-on naturally prevents us from seeing clearly what is right in front of us.

When Virgil first gained his sight back after forty-five years, he struggled to make sense of the reality in front of him. He couldn't judge distances accurately. He had forgotten what certain things looked like. In an absence of recognizable objects, Virgil's attention was drawn to color and movement. He preferred bright yellow school buses and speeding cars over the faces of friends and family. His eyes kept darting from one new revelation to the next and he was unable to stay focused for long. He could not—quite literally—be clear about where he stood in relationship to the objects around him.

Much like Virgil, we are easily distracted by colorful, moving objects. We talk to each other with constant glances down at our iPhones. We have conversations face-to-face while a Bluetooth[8] hangs from our ear. We constantly stop our friends and family midconversation because we have a call coming in. Our attention is perpetually drawn to "what's new," not "what's now." *What are the most recent updates? Who has posted new pictures? Has anyone shared a new link, a new note, or a new wall post? What did I miss while I was in that meeting? Who tried to contact me while I was on the line with someone else?* We can come to feel as though we're constantly missing out on something, which is exactly how Linda Stone described continuous partial attention in the previous chapter. It's almost as though we're living an out-of-body existence.

---

8 I feel the need to point out that a Bluetooth device is not a fashion accessory. It is stunning to me how many people—mostly young men—walk around with them stuck in their ear despite the fact that they aren't even using them. Yes, I can see the value of hands-free communication while driving. I drive "hands free" all the time—it's why God gave me knees. Likewise, if your hands are full—say you're carrying an icebox with a live human heart in one hand and a vial of toxic material in the other—then it is okay to use a Bluetooth. But if these are the not conditions you find yourself in, then at no time, and not under any circumstance, should you be caught wearing such a device.

What does this "out of body" experience do to our sense of self? Dr. Jon Kabat-Zinn, the founder and director of the Stress Reduction Clinic at the University of Massachusetts Medical Center, offers a diagnosis.

> *We lock ourselves into a personal fiction that we already know who we are and where we are going, that we know what is happening—all the while remaining enshrouded in thoughts, fantasies, and impulses, mostly about the past and about the future, about what we want and like, and what we fear and don't like, which spin out continually, veiling our direction and the very ground we stand on.*

Living in an out-of-body fashion, Kabat-Zinn says, creates an artificial understanding of ourselves. Our self-concept becomes "enshrouded" in temporal distractions that can cloud our direction and even make the ground beneath us an untrustworthy place to stand. Kabat-Zinn argues that this is not really living at all, but rather the acting out of a very unsatisfying personal fiction that we inhabit like disembodied spirits. No wonder we're often confused about what we should do with our lives. There can be no clarity of direction without clarity of self. If we don't wake up to our life, warns Kabat-Zinn, we can miss it altogether.

No one else can do this job of waking up for us,
although our family and friends sometimes try
desperately to get through to us, to help us see
more clearly or break out of our own blindness.
When it comes down to it, wherever you go, there
you are. It's your life that is unfolding.

Our lives unfold, moment by moment, and the only way we
can truly experience them is *in the moment*. Being always-on can
thwart awareness of the present moment, keeping our attention
ever focused on the new rather than the now. Endless Facebook-
checking, email-checking, texting, updating, posting—it all
serves in keeping us "disembodied," unable to get a tangible
grip on ourselves in relation to those around us. Rather than
truly living, we're simply *reacting* to whatever colorful objects
happen to flit into our periphery. The missed moments add up,
says Kabat-Zinn. "It's all too easy to remain on something of a
fog-enshrouded, slippery slope right into our graves."

But how do we go about "waking up" to our lives? How do
we make sense of ourselves in a world where we are distracted by
so many colorful, fast-moving objects—especially when many of
those objects are very *good*? How do we go about co-creating in a
world with so many choices? What kind of adaptation is needed
in order to live well in an always-on reality? After all, Sherry Turkle
concludes, "We never 'graduate' from working on identity. We
simply work on it with the materials we have at a particular stage
in life. Online social worlds provide new materials." In short, how
do we go about using our "new materials" to find greater clarity?

Virgil's experience of learning to see again was difficult, even painful. There was much he did not enjoy about it. In many ways, he would have preferred to remain blind, because at least in a nonsighted world, he knew how to operate. But his hard work was worth it. To Virgil's surprise, his difficulties in learning to see again came with a gift that he had not considered in the whole process. In celebration of his first Christmas as a sighted man, Virgil returned to the family farm in Kentucky. He saw his old farmhouse, the fences, the creek, the rolling green pastures he had not seen since he was a child. Most importantly to him, for the first time in forty years, Virgil saw his mother, face-to-face. Sacks reflected on the joyous moment: "Some of [Virgil's] seeing had been a great disappointment, but seeing home and family was not—it was a pure joy."

Adjusting to clear sight after being blind is indeed a challenge. Learning to live in a world of light and clarity instead of shadows and fuzzy shapes takes time. It requires adaptation and a lot of hard work. But as we discover clarity, we also discover the great many unexpected gifts that come with it.

Fortunately for us, a perfect example of how this works is not that far away. In fact it just happens to be hovering about 350 miles overhead.

These unpredictable outcomes require the affected population to adapt their behavior to more adequately live within the new spontaneously generated order.

FIVE
ADAPTATION

"Space," says *The Hitchhiker's Guide to the Galaxy* in a thick British accent, "is big. Really big. You just won't believe how vastly hugely mind-bogglingly big it is. I mean, you might think it's a long way to the chemist, but that's just peanuts to space."

Perhaps no other device has revealed the "really big-ness" of space quite as well as the Hubble Space Telescope. When the Hubble Space Telescope (HST) was first shot into orbit in April 1990, the hopes of the entire astronomical community went with it. Hubble—with its cutting-edge ability to see farther than any earthbound observatory before it—was going to provide an unprecedented glimpse of the universe. For the first time in history, the HST would reveal in pristine photographs the very stuff astronomers and physicists had only theorized. A revolution was coming. There was just one little problem. And that one little problem happened to be the fact that the Hubble Space Telescope was plagued with several hundred *huge* problems that nearly ensured its early demise. The story goes like this.

In 1946, Lyman Spitzer first proposed his idea of a "space telescope." A space-based telescope, Spitzer argued, would be able to out-see any observatory on Earth because it would be free from the natural visual distortions created by Earth's atmosphere. Step outside the atmosphere, he confidently proclaimed, and you step outside the limits of what we now know about the universe. But it was another twenty years before Spitzer found an audience for his ideas. In 1964 the National Academy of Science asked Spitzer to head up their blandly named "Ad Hoc Committee on the Large Space Telescope." Three years after that, Spitzer and his committee published their findings and urged the scientific community to begin seeking out ways to turn the concept of a space-based telescope into a reality. NASA, which had been working on the idea simultaneously, decided to join ranks with the NAS, and in 1971 proposed a budget for the construction of the world's firsts space telescope. Unfortunately the estimated cost of half a billion dollars made the project a tough sell. It was another six years before Congress finally agreed to finance the operation. Once the budget was approved, however, the initial development and construction began quickly, and NASA made plans to launch the space telescope in 1983.

Almost immediately things came to yet another screeching halt. The Perkin-Elmer Corporation had finished the mirror section of the telescope in 1981, but the entire optical assembly was not completed until 1984. The craft's final assembly was not finished for another year, forcing Hubble to be rescheduled for launch in 1986. The HST program was already three years behind when it experienced yet another setback: On January 28, the space shuttle *Challenger* blew up a minute after launch, a tragedy witnessed by millions around the world that killed seven astronauts and scrubbed NASA's shuttle flights for two years. In 1988, NASA set a new date for the space telescope's launch, and in 1990, much to the relief and delight of the massive design and construction team—some of whom had now been involved with the program for *decades*—the Hubble Space Telescope made its way out of Earth's atmosphere and set up orbit 350 miles above the planet.

It had taken *forty-five years* and billions of dollars in research, development, and construction for Lyman Spitzer's idea to become a working reality. Unfortunately, "working" was exactly what the HST seemed *not* to be doing.[1]

Like London's Millennium Bridge, the Hubble Space Telescope's "grand opening" was followed by an immediate shutdown. Why? It turned out the HST's primary mirror—the very system the entire craft was designed around—had been incorrectly manufactured. Specifically, the edges of the mirror had been "ground too flat." Like Virgil, the HST's main "eye" had been "born" with visual distortions that NASA politely referred

---

1 Also unfortunate, it seemed, was the fact that Spitzer did not get his name on the technology he had inspired and largely developed. That's because NASA does not name their telescopes after people still living. Fortunately (or unfortunately, depending on how you look at it), Spitzer died in 1997, earning him a telescope with his name on it. The Spitzer Space Telescope—the fourth and final in a series of "Great Observatories" launched by NASA—found its way into orbit in 2003.

to as "a spherical aberration." The Hubble Telescope, it seemed, was turning out to be as ornery and unpredictable as the man it was named after.

Edwin Hubble was born in 1889 in Missouri, and grew up there and in Illinois. His father had become quite successful in insurance, so money was never really a problem for Hubble and his family. In addition, Hubble was reportedly a "strong and gifted athlete, charming, smart, and immensely good looking." Hubble studied physics and astronomy at the University of Chicago and was accepted as one of the first Rhodes scholars to Oxford University. At age thirty he took a job at the Mount Wilson Observatory in Los Angeles and eventually made a name for himself as "the most outstanding astronomer of the 20th century." According to Bill Bryson in his delightful and detailed book *A Short History of Nearly Everything*, Hubble "seemed too good to be true." In fact it turned out that Hubble was exceedingly arrogant and a compulsive liar, manufacturing stories about his accomplishments and abilities at will. Though it was Hubble who first proved the universe was much, much bigger than anyone previously imagined, and that it was continuing to expand at a steady rate, he remained almost entirely ignorant of the work of his contemporary Albert Einstein.

Einstein's General Theory of Relativity was a perfect complement to what Hubble was discovering and would have strengthened science's grasp on the universe, but he refused to pay any attention. He was consumed with his own work and reputation within the scientific community and felt he could not be bothered. Oddly, Bryson notes, when Hubble died of a heart attack in 1953, his wife "declined to have a funeral and never revealed what she did with the body." To this day, "the whereabouts of the 20th century's greatest astronomer remain unknown." Hubble, it seemed, was cursed despite all of his promise and potential, a form of bad luck he may have passed on to the massive space telescope that would come to bear his name.

Further adaptation was required by the HST teams to get it into proper working order. So in 1993 a combination of repair crews was finally sent to fix Hubble's primary mirror and restore its vision. The five-day mission was successful and the Hubble Space Telescope immediately began to transmit back photographs of the pristine quality astronomers and physicists had always hoped to see. But the 1993 "fix" was only the first of a half-dozen similar repair missions to come in its nearly twenty years of operation. During that time, the future of the HST was again placed in question after yet another shuttle disaster—this time the *Columbia* in 2003—caused NASA to scrub ongoing repairs and retrofitting.

In addition, each repair mission proved both immensely challenging and dangerous, the risk of failure or death compounding with each new attempt to improve on the HST's design. Fixing the HST, after all, is like fixing any other mechanical object: You need tools and you need access to the object. In space this means you've got to do what NASA refers to as an EVA: Extra-vehicular activity. That's "space walking" to folks like you and me. And space-walking comes with its own set of risks and challenges.

Take the EVA suit ("spacesuit"), for example. This time-tested piece of equipment is much more than a couple of oxygen tanks strapped to an astronaut's back. It has its own complicated air-treatment system that filters out harmful carbon dioxide and provides the astronaut just the right amount of oxygen. It has its own battery pack to run lights and communication equipment, and an onboard computer system that monitors the astronaut's physiology as well as its own structural integrity. Since space is mostly a very, very cold place, and cold hands make delicate repairs difficult if not impossible, EVA suits come equipped with "finger heaters" that can be controlled by the astronauts while they are working. An average space walk lasts six hours so the EVA suits come equipped with a drinking tube to keep the astronauts hydrated. However, they do not come with their own sewage system, so spacewalkers must wear what is informally known as a "space diaper."

In all, the EVA suit is a remarkable piece of equipment that allows a human to adapt to the unfriendly conditions of space. But it is not bulletproof. Or more accurately, it is not micro-meteorite proof. This is a significant issue because, as the astronauts go about their delicate repairs outside the spacecraft, they are also zipping through space at around eighteen thousand miles per hour. NASA once tested the effects of a collision between a small metal fragment and a stationary object at this speed. The impact from a tiny quarter-inch steel ball blew a three-inch-wide hole in a half-inch steel plate. Imagine, then, what a small bit of space debris would do to an EVA suit and the unfortunate soul who happened to be wearing it at the time.

In spite of the dangers of repairing the Hubble, the HST teams have always considered the risks to be worth its ability to let us see farther and more clearly into the universe than ever before. Greg Harbaugh, an astronaut who performed Hubble repairs during a pair of space walks in 1997, said affectionately, "It is probably the greatest instrument or tool for astronomical and astrophysical research since Galileo invented the telescope." In fact the clarity introduced by the Hubble Space Telescope has forced the scientific community to rethink their ideas of the universe altogether.

Take for example, the interesting notion of "dark matter." The idea of dark matter has been around since 1933 when Fritz Zwicky,[2] a Swiss astrophysicist at Cal Tech, first proposed the idea. The visible universe, made up of planets, stars, gases, etc., represents only about 4 percent of what is actually out there. Zwicky hypothesized the idea in an attempt to explain not only where "the rest of the universe" had gotten to but also why galaxies seemed to behave the way they do. Galaxies, Zwicky observed, spun and held together in a way that no visible source of gravity could explain. Thus, there must be dark matter in the universe that has enough gravitational force of its own to cause galaxies to act the way they do. In other words, Zwicky concluded, dark matter is the glue that holds galaxies together.

It was forty years before the scientific community started buying into Zwicky's idea. But it wasn't until the invention of the Hubble Space Telescope that astrophysicists could see far

---

2 For the record, Fritz Zwicky is his real name, not his "Jedi name."

enough and clearly enough to determine that, yes, something is out there that explains galactic behavior and, yes, it cannot be seen (though its effects can). At the same time, also thanks to the Hubble, they soon found that dark matter only makes up another 24 percent of the known universe. Even including the 4 percent that could be seen, there was still a lot of universe to be accounted for. What of the other 72 percent?

With the help of the Hubble Space Telescope (among other technologies), scientists were able to piece together another strange but compelling idea: the existence of "dark energy."[3] It was Hubble himself who had first proposed the idea of an expanding universe. The telescope that bore his name helped the scientific community determine that, not only was the universe expanding, but its expansion was *accelerating*.

This gave rise to the idea of dark energy as a way of explaining the force that causes the accelerating expansion of the universe. In addition, the idea helped account for most of the "missing" universe—it is believed that nearly two-thirds of the universe is composed of dark energy. In both cases the new information relayed by the Hubble Space Telescope forced astrophysicists to adapt the way they thought about the universe, and that is no small feat.

The Hubble Space Telescope has been scheduled for decommission in or around 2013 to be replaced by a new kid on the

---

3 "Dark" matter and "dark" energy share nothing in common except for the word "dark." "Dark" simply refers to the fact that they can't be seen—only their effects can be seen. The short answer to why they are unrelated lies in the fact that one is matter and one is energy. For a longer answer, visit www.hubblesite.org.

block, the Webb Telescope.[4] In spite of all the challenges its designers and builders had to overcome, the HST achieved its mission of helping us "see" the universe in a way that we had previously only imagined in our mind's eye. It brought an unprecedented clarity to the study of astronomy and physics that, in turn, has revolutionized the way we think about our universe.

Think back to the case of the Millennium Bridge. We discovered three realities that shaped the events of its opening day. First, "there is a force that is capable of synchronizing a large population in very little time, thereby creating *spontaneous order*." Such was the case when the *footfalls* of several hundred pedestrians created vibrations in the bridge that spread and multiplied until, finally, the entire structure began wobbling like an old metal saw. Second, "spontaneous order can generate outcomes that are entirely new and unpredictable." The two-hundred-person bridge design team—representing some of the best engineering minds in the world—had not been able to predict the "wobbling" effect that was generated when the pedestrians made their inaugural journey across the bridge. Despite all their best efforts, even the experts hadn't seen it coming. Now in the final

---

4 The Webb Telescope, which is scheduled for launch in 2013, will reportedly sit out in space one million miles from Earth, sending back pictures of even higher quality and vaster distances than the HST.

section of this book, we come to the *third* reality revealed by the events of the Millennium Bridge's opening day:

> *These unpredictable outcomes require the affected population to adapt their behavior to more adequately live within the new spontaneously generated order.*

In the case of the Millennium Bridge, pedestrians had to adapt to a different manner of walking in order to accommodate the newly swaying bridge—they were forced to take on a "skating gait" if they were to make their way safely across. Likewise, the new discoveries made by the Hubble Space Telescope forced astronomers and physicists to adapt to a new way of thinking about the universe. They had to come to terms with a universe that was not only accelerating in its expansion but was mostly composed of material that was invisible. In a similar fashion the new "spontaneous order" of Facebook is forcing us to adapt. More specifically, as the experience of human relationships becomes increasingly composed of time spent with others online, we have to (1) adapt the way we think of community and (2) adapt the way we live in community. We're going to explore each adaptation in turn, and we'll begin with a little eavesdropping on a conversation already in progress.

In early 2009 a friendly showdown took place among three leading Christian thinkers and writers over the subject: *What is community and can it really be found online?* They all took a turn arguing their point in an effort to clarify the matter. The conversation began with Shane Hipps. Hipps is currently the lead pastor for Trinity Mennonite Church in Phoenix, Arizona, but his early career was in advertising and marketing, an experience he points to as the source for his passion to understand and clarify the interplay between culture and technology.[5] In a brief video interview for *Christianity Today*'s popular blog, Out of Ur, Hipps referred to the concept of *virtual community*, saying, "It's virtual, but it ain't community." Hipps went on to explain. "Meaningful, missional Christian community should have several ingredients. One is a kind of shared history together … shared history helps establish a sense of identity and belonging. The second is permanence—permanence is how you *get* a shared history. Next, you need proximity—you have to *be* with one another in order to create the kind of meaningful connections [needed] to have community. And then, last, I would say there's a 'fourth ingredient': a shared imagination of the future—a sense of 'we're all going in the same direction.'" Hipps points out that this "fourth ingredient" is "the hardest one to get" because of the challenges that stem from the first three.

---

5 Hipps is the author of the recent *Flickering Pixels: How Technology Shapes Your Faith* and his 2006 book, *The Hidden Power of Electronic Culture: How Media Shapes Faith, the Gospel, and Church.*

As most of us have experienced at one time or another, living in full agreement with friends or family members is a rare experience. Mostly we tend to *disagree* about what matters most and how to live accordingly. But, Hipps said, the notion of "online community" is changing all of that (or at least giving the appearance of change). "In real, unmediated human communities a shared imagination is the hardest one to get. What's fascinating is *online* community gets you that fourth ingredient fastest, easiest, immediately, but *denies* the other three. The reason you interact with online community is that they already believe the kinds of things you're interested in." Hipps explained that, while the experience of "shared imagination" one can find in virtual community is marginally satisfying, it is also mostly a "disembodied" encounter with another. Hipps questioned whether this out-of-body style of relating could truly achieve what we long for in our experience of community. "You do get a shared sense of the future and that's great. Enjoy it! But don't call it community."

Hipps's interview brings up some excellent questions. Does online community really satisfy our relational needs? Can there be an experience of authentic community without face-to-face interaction? What are the consequences of spending more and more time relating online and less frequent time relating in person?

Hipps's response to those questions represents an assumption commonly held that there is something called "real" community and quite another thing called "online" or "virtual" community. This assumption presupposes that the two are very different in terms of quality and style, and that one ("real") is certainly better than the other ("virtual"). While Hipps is right on the money in describing the benefits of "real" relationships, the problem is that his is an assumption shared by fewer and fewer of us in the Facebook universe. To us, the real and the virtual are intertwined.

Scot McKnight has witnessed this firsthand. McKnight is an internationally recognized authority on "the historical Jesus" and a professor of religious studies at North Park University in Chicago. He has written more than twenty books and leads an online community through his blog, The Jesus Creed. McKnight responded to Hipps's interview a few days after it appeared on Out of Ur. "Your point about not equating virtual community with real community is one that needs to be heard," says McKnight. "But I'm not sure it is this simple." McKnight went on to explain, "For some, this blog (The Jesus Creed) is about the only 'community' with Christians they can have right now. I honor that. For others it is therapeutic to dance, as it were, at a distance—not the complete thing, of course, but still participating in some dimensions of community. And there is another dimension: there are clearly dimensions of fellowship at work in blog communities."

McKnight went on to describe helpful interpersonal exchanges that he has experienced via email, pointing to the fact that even those "disembodied" interactions can be meaningful for both him and those he connects with online. "By shrinking community to 'embodied' community, I wonder if we have written 'communion of the saints' (also a community) off the map. Isn't there something eternal, something spiritual, and something profoundly true that all Christians of all ages and of all locations are in communion with one another?" Finally, McKnight observes, "I wonder if it is not swinging too far the other way to deny the word 'community' to what can happen— palpably so for many—in cyberspace."

Both Hipps and McKnight seemed to agree that meaningful community—whether virtual or real—contains certain elements: a level of openness and honesty, for one, and an ongoing participation in the relationship, for another. But they seemed to disagree over the *value* of such exchanges, implying that, in most minds, there is still a distinction between "real" and "online" relationships. This again represents what those "born digital" would likely think of as an artificial distinction between real and online community. On their terms there is no such thing as "community" without both.

Anne Jackson is the author of *Mad Church Disease* and a popular speaker who runs a blog called flowerdust.net. About a week after McKnight responded to Hipps's video interview, Jackson added her voice to the "What is community and can we really find it online?" conversation on Out of Ur. She wrote,

Blogging. Facebook. Twitter. Those three things are practically my middle name. During my four years as the leader of a very thriving blog, I've seen many incredible things happen. I've seen believers and unbelievers unite in generously donating close to $200,000 to social justice and poverty.

I've seen people openly discuss taboo subjects: por-
nography, depression, anxiety, gay lifestyles, and
theologically grey topics. The platforms of social
media certainly give these personal interactions a
"jump start" so to speak, because you do, in some
regard, know bits and pieces of the other person's
life. But this is where it gets muddy for me. Is it
community?

Jackson admitted that, despite her thriving blog and the many significant online interactions she has experienced with others, the question of whether online community is "real community" or not was difficult to answer. She continued, "I believe what happens online is *connection*—not *community*. People can be vulnerable and honest online. And at times these online connections can be more life-giving than many of our offline relationships, but they are not the same." What's particularly interesting about Jackson's assessment is that it hearkens back to Seligman's study about what makes people happy. According to him, the answer was "connection." Could the connection Jackson addresses have the same quality as Seligman's?

Jackson, like Hipps and McKnight before her, acknowledged that online exchanges could be—and often *are*—meaningful for the people involved. But Jackson also observed that, "When we spend more time staring at a glowing monitor than we do into the eyes of those we love, or need to love, it might be time to shut off the computer." In a bold attempt to answer for herself whether or not "online life gets in the way of … offline life,"

Jackson submitted herself to a "Facebook fast." In addition to
putting a freeze on her Facebook and Twitter use, she also shut
her blog down for forty days as a way of celebrating the Lenten
season prior to Easter.[6]

But Jackson's verbal response (and her brave temporary
change of lifestyle) did not constitute the last thread of conversation around "What is virtual community?" For that, Hipps
*re*appeared on the Our of Ur blog to respond to—in case you're
keeping score at home—the *response* of the *response* to Hipps's
original claim that "it might be virtual, but it ain't community."
"When I say that 'virtual community' is not 'community,'"
clarified Hipps,

> *that does not mean it has no value. I know that
> all kinds of deeply meaningful connections and
> interactions happen online all the time. I have
> experienced them myself. I just don't call it "com-
> munity." In my opinion, one is actually better
> than the other. The reason is that "virtual com-
> munity" occurs primarily on one frequency of the
> human experience: it is mostly a disembodied,
> and largely cognitive, connection. And that's won-
> derful; it's a good thing. It's just not as valuable
> as unmediated community, which involves the
> entire range of the human experience—physical,*

---

6 As of this writing, Jackson was still in the thick of her "Facebook fast." To find out
what she learned from her experience, visit www.flowerdust.net.

> *non-verbal, intuitive sense, subtle energies, visual*
> *cues, acoustic tones, etc. I guess what I'm saying is*
> *that virtual community is like playing the guitar*
> *with one string. You can make music; it's just not*
> *as interesting or as good as music on a guitar with*
> *six strings.*

Hipps's clarification of his *original* "clarification" seemed to indicate that perhaps all three voices were in fact saying the same thing but seeing the issue through different lenses. In other words, all three were absolutely right: Community certainly requires something more than just disembodied clicks of "add as friend," and at the same time, there's something community-like happening online that deserves to be taken seriously.[7]

Going further, as Hipps, McKnight, and Jackson suggest, the idea that a certain quality of relationship can be nurtured in the real world over and against the virtual world is valid. It's true that when we think of community, we often mean a felt sense of intimate belonging—a place within a group of people that fits our unique nature so well that we literally feel "right at home" or "completely ourselves" among them. And when we "feel right at home," it's almost like returning to a mirror for the first time in a long time: *Oh, that's right. That's what I look like. That's who I am.* So the experience of community we most desire is the experience of coming home and coming back to ourselves.

---

7 Perhaps one of the most striking things about the debate was the fact that it took place in an entirely virtual environment (a blog), an indicator that the way we think of and operate in community is indeed changing.

In light of this, we can see that the conversation between our three bloggers provides a bedrock definition of community that many of us have in common. Ultimately it is difficult if not impossible to feel "at home" and "ourselves" with others apart from the four qualities that Hipps mentioned—a shared history, a sense of permanence, proximity, and a shared imagination for the future. Many of us would say—like Hipps—that this is a "higher quality" of relationship than we can find online, one better suited for our humanity.

But that brings us to the core of the issue: Younger generations, as well as an increasing number of people throughout the lifespan, would say relating in the "real" world is not an experience of either "higher" or "lower" quality, it is simply another way of relating. After all, they have mostly experienced relationships as always having contained a strong online component. Theirs is a world where an intimate conversation is just as likely to take place over email (or on each other's Facebook walls) as in the locker room or a coffeehouse or a church building. Their brand of community can and does happen as easily and as often online as not. In other words, for a growing number of people—especially those from younger generations—"community" is not understood as a dichotomy between "real" or "online" relationships, but as a composite of *both*.

This growing reality forces us to adapt the way we think about community. It is no longer enough to define community in either good or bad terms, to debate whether one brand of relating ("real") is better than another ("online"), though as we saw in chapter three and in the conversations above, there is certainly a qualitative difference between the two. A more inclusive definition is needed, one that takes into account the fact that the always-on do not make traditional distinctions between real and online relationships. Hipps, McKnight, and Jackson have laid a solid foundation. Yes, we are indeed looking for people with whom we can feel "at home" and "ourselves"—that same driving force that has brought a few hundred million into orbit around Facebook. But now let's build on the truths we've found through eavesdropping on their conversation around "What is community?" by adding to it the question of "*Who* is my community?"

Mark Scandrette,[8] executive director of ReIMAGINE, a center for spiritual direction, helps us adapt our ideas of community by sharing from his experience of living within an "intentional community" in San Francisco:

> *I frequently hear people use the phrase "my community" to refer to a special group of people they have chosen to relate to. We sometimes speak of "community" as the illusive and idyllic sense of warmth and connectedness that we long for. But perhaps in actuality most of us have all the "community" we need: neighbors, coworkers, relatives, and friends. Our challenge is to learn to embrace, nurture, and cultivate these relationships to their*

---

8 Scandrette wrote a book called *Soul Grafitti*, an excellent resource for learning how to live authentically within an "always-on" context. You can learn more about Scandrette and his experiences with intentional community by visiting www.reimagine.org.

fullest potential—to become the best kind of neighbor, daughter, uncle, colleague, or friend.

Scandrette's definition of community seems to imply that community is less about "best-friendship" and more about intentional engagement with the people in our lives. These are obviously people with whom we enjoy a certain proximity, true, but Scandrette's definition is nevertheless a subtle but significant shift away from the relational consumerism of "Where can I find a group of people who fit *me?*" According to Scandrette, "Who is my community?" is a question that turns our attention outward and makes us ready to discover community even in unexpected places.

"Where is the community that fits me?" on the other hand, is a question that turns our attention solely to our wants and our personal preferences, a sandy foundation on which to build any kind of relationship (though we typically try anyway). Scandrette acknowledges that we all need close relationships— that we were made for them—but wonders whether that means we must have everything in common. Do we really have to be BFFs to experience community, or might there be more to community than we've grown accustomed to thinking about?

Scandrette's question "*Who* is my community?" highlights the fact that how we behave in community determines our experience of community. If we relate in superficial ways, then we will only experience superficial community. In the same way, if we relate to one another in authentic, life-giving ways, we will experience authentic, life-giving community. If we are unsatisfied with the kind of experience we're having, is it related to our group or to the nature of how we're offering ourselves (or withholding ourselves) to others? These questions imply that how we do community is even more important than where we do community.

As we adapt to a new way of thinking about community, maybe it's not the increasingly "online" nature of our relationships that is affecting our relationships most (though, as we learned in chapter four, it is still significant). Perhaps instead it is our "relational consumerism" that needs changing.

Over the decades, as the Hubble Space Telescope was being dreamed up, designed, built, launched, and repaired, the scientific community was learning a great deal about the environmental impact of space upon space-travelers. In their fascinating book, *Space Psychology and Psychiatry*, authors Nick Kansas and Dietrich Manzey summarized much of what is now known about the effects of living and working in space. They cited two sets of factors as having influence on an astronaut's well-being.

The first set of factors had to do with the physical nature of the space environment. An astronaut's physiology, they observed, is impacted most by two attributes unique to space travel: "microgravity" and the alteration of the natural dark-light cycle. Microgravity (what we often refer to as "weightlessness") proves a challenge to the body's cardiovascular

system (blood circulation), its sensorimotor system (body movement and coordination), and its musculoskeletal systems
(muscle and bone strength). Why? Because our bodies have
developed and adapted according to the gravitational conditions unique to Earth. In the microgravity environment of
space, by comparison, the undisciplined human body begins
to break down.[9]

But the alteration of the body's natural dark-light cycle
is equally punishing. When zipping through space at 18,000
mph, the sun "rises" every ninety minutes (and you thought
your day was short). This is radically different from the twenty-
four-hour day-night cycle we are used to on Earth, so the
body's natural circadian rhythm of sleeping and waking loses
its calibration, creating significant sleep and performance issues
for astronauts.

As if the factors affecting physiological functioning weren't
enough, there is a second set of factors that have psychological
impact on those traveling in space. Listen as they're described
by Kansas and Manzey:

> *The second set of factors contributing to*
> *space as an extreme environment for humans*
> *is related to the numerous habitability, psy-*
> *chological and interpersonal stressors during*
> *space flight. These result from the harsh living*

---

9 This effect was humorously demonstrated in the computer-animated Pixar film
WALL-E, where Earth's remaining survivors had all grown immensely obese, weak, and
uncoordinated after long years of space travel aboard the Axiom.

conditions in a space habitat, the restricted range of environmental cues ... and the psychosocial situation that is often characterized by a lack of privacy, enforced social contacts with other crew members, and separation from the usual social network of family and friends. Most of these factors are not specific for space flight conditions but are universal for confined and isolated environments. Yet they represent important aspects of long-duration space flight. Similar to the unique physical conditions of the space environment, they represent stressors which astronauts have to adapt to.

Kansas and Manzey described how, in order to adapt to the rigors of a space environment, special sleeping arrangements had to be made. Artificial "days" and "nights" had to be established. Eating and exercise routines required highly detailed monitoring and management. And that was just to take care of the astronaut's bodies. To care for their psyche in space required yet another long list of adaptations, including attitude and behavior changes. But what Kansas and Manzey demonstrated as the unique experience of working and living in space can be just as easily applied to what we're finding in the always-on environment of cyberspace: In order to live well in a challenging environment, we have to adapt our thinking and our behavior.

In an interview with Eric Hurtgen for *Relevant* magazine, Dallas Willard explored how an always-on culture like Facebook shapes the way we relate to one another.

> *People identify life with consuming … and not just consuming stuff you might buy in a store but consuming all the stuff that is offered to them. They are constantly being hammered with all types of things which they open themselves up to by staying plugged in. The old saying from the drug generation, "Tune in, turn on, and drop out" has been made manifest, we have a generation of young people now who are living in a constant state of "dropped out-ness" from the real world and from its history and from community and from the integrity of themselves.… And they don't even know that.*

Willard's comments initially seemed a bit grandfatherly (a pardonable offense since he is, in fact, a grandfather) and (the much younger) Hurtgen responded accordingly: "But you're talking about a generation that has put a great amount of emphasis on having friends and surrounding themselves with community." Willard explained:

> *That's an expression of their loneliness. But most of them don't know what community means because*

community means assuming responsibility for
other people and that means paying attention
and not following your own will but submitting
your will and giving up the … little consumer
world that you have created. They are lonely and
they hurt. They don't know why that they think
community might solve that, but when they look
community in the face and realize that it means
raw, skin to skin contact with other people for
whom you have become responsible … that's
when they back away. See, [human] brokenness
manifests itself as an inability for people to do
what they know to be right, and the ability to
do what you know to be right is a prerequisite for
true community.

Willard's view of community is almost a slap in the face to the popular culture of Facebook. Responsibility for one another? Submitting our will and giving up the "little consumer world" we have created for ourselves? The "ability to do what's right is a prerequisite for true community"? We might be tempted to ask, "How old *is* this guy?" But upon reflection, Willard's comments bring an intense Hubble-like clarity to "community," one that forces us to adapt not only the way we think of community but also how we act in community.

As Willard observes, we seek satisfying relationships as an expression of our loneliness. We might also say that "loneliness" is our human need for "home"—that heartfelt desire for a safe, intimate space where we can belong. But there is no experience of "home" where all parties involved are not mutually blessing each other, that is, submitting and taking responsibility for one another.

A good marriage is an example of how this works. In a good marriage a person enjoys the safety, intimacy, and freedom of home while simultaneously offering those same gifts to the other. The gifts are not offered in response to the other's affection. Rather they are the very means by which the two people relate to one another.

In the same way, it is impossible to experience satisfying community without this cycle of continual gift-bearing and gift-receiving. We can't "enjoy home" without being able to "offer home" at the same time. This in fact is the nature of co-creating. And that brings us to the heart of the matter: In order to experience the quality of relationships we long for, we have to take personal responsibility for the way we relate to one another. That implies that personal maturity is required, or what Willard calls "the ability to do what we know to be right."

Personal maturity means the ability to know and do the right thing, even when we don't feel like it. After all, the elements that make home safe and satisfying—learning to compromise, sharing the household duties, resolving conflicts, sticking together—are the very elements we'd naturally rather avoid.

Children may "play house" and pretend to be married, but—as we should expect of children—they are incapable of the emotional maturity required to imagine a real marriage or home. Yet what we expect of children has come to be what we expect of adults, as well. It is more likely that we'd prefer to "play house" than submit ourselves to the rigors (and pleasures) of mutually blessing community. We'd rather be consumers of relationships—taking the parts we want and leaving out the parts we don't—than face dealing with all of home's demands (and benefits). And so, unfortunately, we scratch our heads and wonder why we can't seem to find the kind of community experience we're looking for, all the while remaining willfully adolescent in our relational habits.

Few environments illustrate this pattern as well as Facebook. Like Andrew Wallenstein noted in the previous chapter (just before he encountered Bob the stalker), a Facebook friendship "really isn't too demanding of a relationship." Our Facebook connections typically require little thought or action on our part. We don't have to work hard at them, or offer much of ourselves in return. We don't have to "take responsibility" for anyone. We get to enjoy glimpses into our friends' lives—both old and new—without all that messy "getting to know you" business. And perhaps most importantly to us, we get to reveal and withhold whatever we feel like. We are in control. We do not answer to anything other than our own temporal wishes. Which is how we can end up with little more than what Hipps called that "fourth ingredient"—a shared vision for the future (i.e., a place where people tend to believe and value the same things we do)—but miss out on the other three: the sense of identity and belonging that come from a shared history, the safety found in a sense of permanence, and the intimacy that accompanies proximity. We get a sip of home even as we grow increasingly thirsty for home.

So we need a change. Like space travelers, we have to adapt our thinking and our behavior to accommodate the rigors of our new always-on environment. We have to shelve old ways of thinking and old ways of living and enter into a new co-created reality that will enable us to thrive in a hyperconnected world. What would it look like to do this?

Hopefully you still have some of that sunscreen left, because we'll need to make one final trip to the desert in order to find out.

SIX
REGENERATION

For more than two thousand years, people have been trying to get their minds around the person of Jesus. Even within the church (*especially* within the church), people have debated Jesus' integrity, His identity, and His legacy. There is, however, at least one thing that stands out in the gospel accounts of the life of Jesus that leaves little room for debate. "Jesus was a friend of sinners," writer Philip Yancey observed. "They liked being around him and longed for his company. Meanwhile, legalists found him shocking, even revolting. What was Jesus' secret that we have lost?"

The gospel of John records the story of Jesus meeting the woman at the well. Jesus had been traveling from Judea to Galilee, and much to his disciples' surprise, decided to pass through Samaria. Any respectable Jew would have normally taken great pains to avoid Samaria, even though it lay directly in the path between Judea and Galilee. But, John writes, that's exactly what Jesus did, ending up at a watering hole called Jacob's Well.

"Jesus, tired as he was from the journey, sat down by the well. It was about noon" (John 4:6). As Jesus was sitting and resting (His disciples had gone off to buy food), a Samaritan woman came along to draw water from the well and Jesus asked her for a drink. And what at first seemed like a mundane detail—Jesus is thirsty and asks for a drink—turned out to be an absolutely scandalous act.

The woman was, in the first place, a woman, and men did not typically speak casually with women in that culture. To do so would have created suspicion about the man's intentions. Second, the woman was a Samaritan, and as we've already noted, Jews never associated with Samaritans. Interacting with Samaritans was a shameful act for Jews, because they thought of Samaritans as unclean, contaminated people. And third, the woman just happened to be a known adulterer who had had many husbands and lovers. Imagine the shock of seeing a respected religious leader of that time striking up a conversation with a woman of such ill repute, in broad daylight.

Adding to the scandal was the fact that the woman drew water from the well at noon. Water was typically drawn in the early morning to avoid the scorching midday sun, but this woman arrived at noon. Why? Quite simply, the woman was drawing water in the brutal heat of midday to avoid the shame of running into her neighbors. The biblical account suggests that many people in town knew her story and gossiped about her latest escapades as though she were the Samaritan Britney Spears. So the woman made her way to the well at noon. And right in the middle of her routine, in the middle of her shame, in the middle of her ongoing search for love, Jesus showed up. "Will you give me a drink?" He asked (v. 7).

The woman was stunned and said, "You are a Jew and I am a Samaritan woman. How can you ask me for a drink?" (v. 9). Jesus, unafraid of what people might think, struck up a conversation with a Samaritan woman, and said plainly, "Everyone who drinks this water will be thirsty again, but those who drink the water I give them will never thirst. Indeed, the water I give them will become in them a spring of water welling up to eternal life" (vv. 13–14).

Jesus gives her a little space to take things in, to respond in a way that was natural for her. She considers His offer and He does not rush her. We can almost hear her mind churning, weighing the benefits, calculating the risks of sticking around to talk to this man. She knew her thirst was both physical and emotional. Samaria was a rocky, hilly region of desert that bordered the hottest, driest part of Israel. Thirst was not a pretty metaphor to her. It was part of her lived reality.

In addition, surely the woman recognized in herself an emotional thirst for loving acceptance, for community, for companionship. Perhaps she was tired of her husband-chasing, crowd-avoiding, water-drawing routine. Did the woman wonder: *What if the "living water" Jesus offered meant she wouldn't have to be lonely again?*

What's more, Jesus identifies Himself with her thirst: He was tired and He sat down by the well, hoping for something cool to drink. Just like her. The simple move seems to win her confidence. Finally, she decides. "Sir, give me this water so that

I won't get thirsty and have to keep coming here to draw water" (v. 15).

And just when it seemed to be like that part of a movie where the orchestra swells dramatically and everything resolves in a beautiful, tear-jerking moment, Jesus says, "Go, call your husband and come back" (v. 16).

Um …

We can imagine the woman flinching, wondering if she had just opened herself up to another man only to be humiliated. "I have no husband," she said (v. 17).

"You are right when you say you have no husband," Jesus agrees. "The fact is, you have had five husbands, and the man you now have is not your husband. What you have just said is quite true" (vv. 17–18).

Why did Jesus bring up the fact that the woman had been married five times and was now living with a man who was not her husband? Was He trying to shame her? Was He just showing off, flaunting a little of his all-knowing-ness? Had Jesus read the local Samaritan tabloids that plastered her erratic behavior on their front pages?

When speaking of the miracles Jesus performed to illustrate His present and future rule, N. T. Wright said,

> *His healings were the sign of a radical and heal-*
> *ing inclusivism—not simply including everyone*
> *in a modern, laissez-faire, anything-goes fash-*
> *ion but dealing with the problems at the root*
> *so as to bring to birth a truly renewed, restored*

community whose new life would symbolize
and embody the kingdom of which Jesus was
speaking.

Jesus was not interested in a relationship with the woman based on false modesty, church niceties, or piety. He was interested in "dealing with problems at the root" in order to offer her a brand-new "community." He wanted to show her a relationship rooted in authenticity. Let's be honest with each other, said Jesus. Let's see things as they really are and build on that. Let's not play games and pretend.

In His unexpected response to the woman, Jesus also managed to speak to the very heart of the human condition. For we, like the Samaritan woman, want to be loved and accepted exactly as we are. No, Jesus did not bring up the woman's history to shame her. He was making it clear that He knew her, He knew what she'd done and what she was doing in the present, and He still wanted to be in a relationship with her.

The woman was stunned by Jesus' words once more. Had she heard Him correctly? Jesus has just detailed her sordid past, but didn't seem to be mocking her for it. And He wasn't walking away, either. What could He be up to? She stammered, unsure where to go, wanting to change the subject. In response to Jesus' honesty, she started babbling about places of worship and where Jews and Samaritans differ in the matter. We, like her, often struggle to know what to do when confronted by unconditional love. It can make us hem and haw. It can make us speechless. It can even make us run for the door. But somehow the woman remained. She stayed with the conversation, as silly as it sounded, a move that would soon change her entire life.

With grace and patience, Jesus didn't change the subject. He let the Samaritan woman steer the conversation according to her own wants and needs and entered in exactly there. "You Samaritans worship what you do not know; we worship what we do know, for salvation is from the Jews," Jesus said. "Yet a time is coming and has now come when the true worshipers will worship the Father in the Spirit and in truth" (John 4:22–23). The woman had changed the subject and Jesus had gone with her. Like a great jazz musician, He deftly improvised among the clunky chords she laid down, turning them into something beautiful and captivating—something worth listening to. Jesus joyfully, creatively engaged her right where she was, even as she made one last attempt to shake Him. "I know that Messiah is coming," she said. "When he comes, he will explain everything to us" (v. 25).

And just then, Jesus revealed Himself to His new friend. "I, the one speaking to you—I am he" (v. 26).

The story to this point has plenty of interesting twists in the plot. We can imagine Hollywood might be able to do some-thing interesting with this scene. But the real twist comes just a few verses further. "Then, leaving her water jar, the woman went back to the town and said to the people, 'Come, see a man who told me everything I ever did. Could this be the Messiah?'" (vv. 28–29).

How is it that a woman who is so ashamed of herself that she takes great pains to avoid her neighbors by going to draw water during the hottest part of the day now drops her water jar, runs into town, and starts bragging about the fact that her past has been exposed? Because when people encounter the kind of intentionality, humility, and authenticity Jesus demonstrated at the well, people get changed.

Facebook, we could say, is a well where thirsty people come to take a drink. We are thirsty for the kind of community where we can feel at home and like ourselves. It is a place where we experience enough of an emotional buzz to keep us coming back, even though we grow increasingly thirsty with every visit. And so habituated are we to our water-gathering routine (being always-on), that it is becoming increasingly difficult to imagine any other way; isn't this the best we can do?

There are three things that stand out from the story of Jesus and the woman at the well. First, Jesus' intentionality set the stage for a life-changing encounter with the woman. Second, Jesus' humility allowed Him to meet her where she was at, without a hint of off-putting pride. And third, Jesus' authenticity allowed Him to establish a genuine relationship with the woman, free from pretense and playacting. These same three elements—intentionality, humility, and authenticity—are going to become our tools in the work of co-creating our Facebook worlds.

Intentionality

Jesus' passage through Samaria wasn't the result of bad maps or poor planning. It was an intentional decision. The conversation Jesus began with the woman was not an accident, either. Yes, He was tired and thirsty and needed a drink of water. But He knew exactly what He intended from the conversation even before He asked, "Will you give me a drink?" Throughout the Gospels we discover in fact that everything Jesus did was intentional. He was intentional in the ways He thought, spoke, and acted—in His personal life as well as His public life.

Intentional living simply means on-purpose living. When an Olympic biathlete bellies up to a snowbound target and takes aim with her rifle, she *intends* to hit the center of that target. Her intention to hit the target sets the stage for the way she arranges her body, holds her rifle, how she takes into account the wind speed and direction, and how she determines the best time and fashion in which to take the shot. Our intentions help us choose the best ways to live (think, speak, and act) in the now and the now-to-come, in order to hit the target. They help determine our goals, how we arrange the circumstances of our lives (as much as we are able) to meet those goals, and the attitude we have in reaching for those goals.

Significantly, there is no such thing as an *un*intentional life. All of us have, at times, felt like we were "drifting through life" or "wandering aimless." Perhaps that's exactly where we find ourselves in this moment. It is a common experience—especially in certain seasons of life[1]—but it does not mean we do not have intentions. It simply means we are not conscious of our intentions. We are not aware of them, even though they are present and determining the direction of our lives as much as a well-thought-out list of goals. This is what is meant by the old saying, "Those who fail to plan, plan to fail." When we are not aware of our intentions, we find that passivity and restlessness (most often in the form of boredom) take root and sprout up like weeds, covering over a clear life path until we are thoroughly lost.

The great challenge in being always-on, of course, is that it rarely enables us to be consciously intentional. More often than not, it thwarts on-purpose living by creating in us a need to respond to what is most urgent rather than what is most valuable. In other words, our hyperconnectivty can lead to hyperreactivity.

For example, Melissa is twenty six years old and works in marketing for Google at its main campus in Mountain View, California. She is new to the area and desires to find new friends but struggles to find the time or energy to do so. Before she gets out of bed in the morning, she reaches over to the nightstand and sleepily grabs her iPhone. Eyes hardly focusing, she checks her email to see if there are any work messages. Then she checks Facebook and updates her status: "Sleepy, but

---

1 Adolescence and young adulthood, for example, are typified by a sense of "wandering" as individuals wrestle to make sense of self, vocation, and relationships, trying on different forms of each. Midlife is another season known for its tendency toward personal reevaluation that can generate an increased sense of restlessness and uncertainty about identity and life direction.

gotta go to work." She hits the ground running. Her day is filled with a seemingly endless number of emails, an ever-lengthening to-do list, and an ever-ringing iPhone, all of which need to be taken care of right now. She woke up feeling behind. By the time she gets home, she feels even more behind. Exhausted, but bored (and a little lonely), she spends a couple of hours before bed surfing the Web, scrolling through Facebook, and answering both work and personal emails in between. She climbs into bed and, just before turning out the lights, does a final email check on her iPhone, along with one last status update. "Exhausted," she thumbs. She falls asleep wondering if her life is going in the direction she wants it to.

For Melissa—and the great many of us she represents—life can all too often feel like little more than a knee-jerk reaction to urgent emails, phone calls, meetings, and decisions. We can start to feel as though we're at the mercy of other people's needs and wants. Our self-care diminishes as our to-do list grows. Our time and energy—even our motivation—gets sapped by the challenges of hyperconnection.

Dallas Willard writes:

> *Now an intention is brought to completion only by a decision to fulfill or carry through with the intention. We commonly find people who say they intend (or intended) to do certain things that they do (or did) not do. To be fair, external circumstances may sometimes have prevented them from carrying out the action. And habits deeply*

rooted in our bodies and life contexts can, for a
while, thwart even a sincere intention. But if
something like that is not the case, we know they
never actually decided to do what they say they
intended to do, and that they therefore did not
really [consciously] intend to do it. They therefore
lack the power and order that intention brings to
the life process.

Our conscious intentions determine our direction. They are our way of "aiming" for what matters most in life. But they do not come easily. The apostle Paul famously (and, I think, rather humorously) put it this way: "I do not understand what I do. For what I want to do I do not do, but what I hate I do.... For I have the desire to do what is good, but I cannot carry it out. For I do not do the good I want to do, but the evil I do not want to do—this I keep on doing" (Rom. 7:15–19). There are a great many reasons why we do not do what we want to do. Very often our intentions are not "brought to completion," as Willard puts it, because of "habits deeply rooted in our bodies and life contexts" that thwart our conscious intentions. Let's look at two of these habits—busyness and procrastination.

There is no question that we are busier than ever, and that our growing connections compound our busyness. Dr. Edward Hallowell, a former Harvard Medical School faculty member and author of the book *CrazyBusy*, said in a *Boston Globe* article, "What we're seeing, we've never seen in human history before. It's just the extraordinary availability and magnetism of electronic communication devices, whether it's cell phones or BlackBerries or the Internet. People tend to—without knowing it or meaning to—spend a lot of time doing what I call 'screen sucking.'" It can feel at times that our technology is managing us and not the other way around. When that feeling turns into a lifestyle of "screen sucking," we find ourselves aiming in the wrong directions. The cost of continuous partial attention rears its ugly head once more.

We cannot live intentionally without being mindful of— aware of, in touch with—our thoughts, feelings, and actions. Mindfulness simply means "paying attention in a particular way: on purpose, in the present moment, and non-judgmentally."

We can see how this works in a very basic example. When we are especially busy, we may forget to eat a meal. It's only when we take a break—when we *tune in* to how we're feeling—that we notice our hunger. Then the thought comes to our mind, *I'm hungry*. We don't say that hunger is good or bad; we simply decide what to do based on what we now notice. Then we run out and buy three pumpkin scones from Starbucks (just me?). In short, busyness is the number-one enemy of mindfulness. Being too busy keeps us from noticing what is going on inside of us, all around us. It's how we can commute to work and not have any memory of passing through certain stoplights. It's how we can have lunch with friends and not remember what they said. It's how we can spend hours on Facebook and then wonder where all of our time went. When our schedules bulge at the seams, we simply cannot live mindfully.

The second habit that thwarts our conscious intentions is procrastination. Why do today what we can put off until tomorrow? The question implies a subtle but sinister bargaining with self. We say things like, "As soon as I get through this deadline. As soon as I break up with my girlfriend. As soon as I get a new job. As soon as I get married, have kids, buy a house, retire." Before long the only option we have is, "As soon as I die." What we gain in the bargaining—a temporary reprieve from some action item—is lost immediately to a growing dissatisfaction with life and an undermining of personal confidence. But very often it seems we don't have a choice in the matter. Many of us live under forced procrastination. We simply cannot keep up with the volume of email or the number of meetings or the things "to-do" and are forced to push them into tomorrow, a practice that makes each new day feel heavier than the last.

The good news is that we have a choice—a myriad of choices, in fact—as to how we will live within our always-on reality. And as we learned in chapter three, our choices give us control over our environment. As such, we can use our intentions to take aim at our goals, to shape a life that is balanced in relationship to the people and technology in our lives. Recent advances in social networking and mobile technology may have opened the door for us to be ever-connected and ever-available to everyone. It may have given us access to our Facebook profile wherever and whenever we want. But we still get to decide what we'll do with that access. At the digital all-you-can-eat buffet, we don't have to stuff ourselves until we throw up.

"Your intentions set the stage for what is possible," says Dr. Jon Kabat-Zinn, founder and director of the Stress Reduction Clinic at the University of Massachusetts Medical Center. Jesus' intentionality set the stage for a personal revolution in the life of the Samaritan woman. It set the stage for a cultural revolution, one that continues right up until this moment. Intentional living is how we participate in, enjoy the benefits of, and further the revolution.

Humility

"Words have enormous power," writes Bruna Martinuzzi, the founder of Clarion Enterprises Ltd., a company that specializes in emotional intelligence and leadership training. "They can make us erupt into laughter or bring tears to our eyes. They can influence, inspire, manipulate and shock. They can build and destroy. Some words have different effects on different people. One such word is humility. It is one of those words that are seldom in neutral gear."

When Jesus spoke to the woman at the well, He met her on her terms. He did not approach her with a holier-than-thou attitude (though He certainly was holier-than-everybody). Out of humility He extended to her a countercultural respect that scandalized everyone. Even His disciples, after returning from their grocery shopping, "were surprised to find him talking to a woman" (John 4:27). Philip Yancey commented on the reason behind Jesus' norm-breaking behavior.

Humility is transformative because it opens us to see beyond our own experience. It allows us to take the wants and needs of others as seriously as we take our own wants and needs. It validates the other even as it validates the self. This means that humility is also transformative because it opens *us* to receive the same regenerative love we show others. This was precisely the experience of the Samaritan woman. She responded to Jesus' humility with a humility of her own: remaining in the conversation despite her own fears ("How can you ask me for a drink?"), telling the truth ("I have no husband"), and opening herself to a new way ("Come, see the man who told me everything I ever did"). The woman's humility-to-humility response allowed her to receive refreshing water even as she offered it to Jesus.

Obviously humility does not mean life as a doormat. Jesus did not allow the great thirst of the woman to prevent Him from asking for what He needed, too ("Give me something to drink"). Humility does not mean we constantly turn a deaf ear to our wants and needs in service of others. True humility always honors both ourselves and others, at the same time. Here the old adage, "You can't love someone else until you love yourself," is very true. We cannot be of any real good to others unless we are simultaneously good to ourselves. Not in a selfish way, mindlessly pursuing whatever new idea or experience might give us pleasure. (This is not love at all—it is merely self-gratification.) Rather, we learn to love ourselves with the same humility and radical inclusiveness that Jesus modeled. This is important because rarely do we treat others as harshly as we treat ourselves. Conversely we will only be able to treat others with as much kindness as we are able to treat ourselves

Of course, a word with the "enormous power" of humility has plenty of enemies. Fear is the most notable. Out of fear we shrink back and hide. We don't want the unlovely parts of us to be seen. We do not want to appear as a student; we'd rather be thought of as a master. To appear calm, cool, and collected— that's our real intention. Out of self-doubt and insecurity, we lose our playful curiosity and become anxious managers of friendships and self-portraits.

Fear is very much part of the climate of Facebook. When we are afraid of what people think of us, we work hard to craft just the right image composed of just the right pictures, personal information, and status updates. We position and reposition the spotlights on our Facebook portraits to reflect our most interesting side. The emphasis is on being clever, not on being genuine. As we've already seen, Facebook, and the Internet in general, rewards those who are most clever, not those with the most character. Unfortunately cleverness has the lifespan of a sickly gnat. Clever ideas, trends, and people pop up then fade away just as quickly. Cleverness has no staying power. As such, it cannot help us live well in a hyperconnected world where what is needed most are qualities that offer permanence and stability. While fear is the illness, it's the symptoms that tend to get our attention—let's look at a few.

Dr. Marshall Rosenberg is the founder and director of educational services for the Center for Nonviolent Communication, an international peacemaking organization. He has spent his life studying and practicing the use of humble, intentional communication as a means for resolving conflict and creating personal transformation. In his book *Nonviolent Communication*, he talks about three ways that a lack of humility prevents us from relating well to one another. The term he uses to describe these forms is "life-alienating communication."

The first form of life-alienating communication, says Dr. Marshall, is *moralistic judgments*. When we say, for example, things like, "That's a dumb status update—he's so self-centered," or, "I can't believe she posted *that* picture," we are making moralistic judgments of others. "When we speak this language," says Rosenberg, "we think and communicate in terms of what's wrong with others for behaving in certain ways, or occasionally, what's wrong with us for not understanding or responding as we would like. Our attention is focused on classifying, analyzing, and determining levels of wrongness rather than on what we and others need and are not getting." Judgment is something the Facebook environment facilitates best. Remember, this is a technology that, in its infancy, asked people to judge who was the "hotter" of two people. Those days are long gone, but it seems the judgmental spirit lingers. For example, the Facebook stream displays our status updates, the latest photos, and shared links like headlines on the front page of a newspaper. In every case people are invited to "comment" or give a "thumbs up." In fact the strength of our Facebook stream grows as we participate in this way. In other words, we are rewarded for our judgments. This is not to say that we shouldn't think critically about our lives, about our friendships, or about the things we post on

Facebook. Of course we should—there is no such thing as a true humility that does not include thinking well. But it does mean that when we move beyond critical thinking into moralistic judgments, we can end up building invisible walls that separate us from others like a Caesar high in his pavilion looking down on the gladiators.

The second form of life-alienating communication that Rosenberg points out is *making comparisons*. Making comparisons is similar to moralistic judgments, but the spotlight is all the more on *us*. In other words, we consciously or unconsciously ask ourselves, "How am I doing in comparison to my Facebook friends?" This is another habit that Facebook makes easy. For one thing, many of us have posted our life experiences like we'd display trophies on a shelf. This isn't all bad—it's good to take pride in our work, play, and relationships. But often we use this information to measure ourselves against others. For example, we can scan a friend's profile to see if their education is better or worse than ours, if their work experience is greater or less, if their earning potential (or, in some cases, actual income) is higher or lower. In addition, pictures of exotic vacations and virtual maps documenting where we've been in the world allow us to see if we are better traveled or not (world travel has long been associated with status in Western culture). We can compare if we're doing better or worse relationally ("single" versus "in a relationship"), if our kids are better or worse looking, if our hairlines have more or less receded. And of course, the number of Facebook friends we have in our list (i.e., the size of our invisible entourage) can lend some status to our profile.

When we peruse each other's Facebook profiles this way, we can reexperience those awful moments when our grades were posted on the teacher's door and we all huddled around to see how we compared to everyone else. It can make us feel depressed and worthless. It can make us feel prideful and better than others. It can also leave us wondering where we stand at all.

The third form of life-alienating communication listed by Rosenberg is *the denial of responsibility*. It is easy in a virtual environment to forget that our words and actions have impact. There is a depersonalizing effect that can happen when we are physically separated from others, and this can create an artificial sense of confidence or a lack of restraint. In this way, depersonalization can lead to dehumanization, and can promote careless and thoughtless Facebooking habits. For example, Christine Rosen, who wrote *Virtual Friendship and the New Narcissism*, related the story of a friend of hers who broke off her engagement. The no-longer bride-to-be had told a few of her friends and family the sad news when a funny thing happened. "Her ex decided to make it official in a very twenty-first century way," said Rosen. "He changed his status on his [Facebook] profile from 'Engaged' to 'Single.' Facebook immediately sent out a feed to every one of their mutual 'friends' announcing the news, 'Mr. X and Ms. Y are no longer in a relationship.'"

Rosen asked her friend how she felt about the matter. Her friend admitted that, while she knew the news would eventually get out, "there was something disconcerting about the fact that everyone found out about it simultaneously; and since the message came from Facebook, rather than in a face-to-face

exchange … it was devoid of context—save for a helpful nota-
tion of the time and that tacky little [broken] heart."

While Rosen's example is out of the norm, it does illustrate
the denial of responsibility most of us assume for our Facebook
behavior. This goes back to our discussion of privacy controls
in chapter four. After all, we often post status updates, links,
and personal information heedless of who it might offend. We
make private meetings on public Facebook walls, regardless of
who may feel left out. We tag photos of ourselves with friends
because we happen to look particularly good in them (regardless
of how our friends come off looking). We are overly cynical,
sarcastic, and even downright mean at times, determined to
express whatever angst is going on inside us at the moment,
unfettered by doubts about the value of such comments. In this
way, Facebook pushes our "monarchy" button and makes us feel
entitled to say and do whatever we feel like in the moment. And
why not? Again, we are mostly rewarded for such behavior. But
"life-alienating" is how Rosenberg described this form of communication and for good reason. When we deny responsibility
for our words or actions—either willfully or carelessly—we
effectively depersonalize our friends, dismissing their thoughts
and feelings as less important than our own. And of course, we
are diminished in the process.

Helen Keller, when reflecting on humility, wrote, "I long
to accomplish great and noble tasks, but it is my chief duty to
accomplish humble tasks as though they were great and noble.
The world is moved along, not only by the mighty shoves of
its heroes, but also by the aggregate of the tiny pushes of each

honest worker." What we find in the life of the Samaritan woman can be true for our experience of Facebook (if we are willing to look): Humility cannot only "move the world along," it can actually turn the world upside down.

Authenticity

In a move that left the Samaritan woman completely shocked, Jesus "told her everything she ever did." He demonstrated the highest form of His respect by offering her a relationship with Him based on who she was, not who she should have been. In addition, Jesus authentically modeled the kind of intentional humility that creates an atmosphere of trust and a potential for change. In doing so, Jesus illustrated the two basic definitions of authenticity, both of which will help us better understand how to live well in an always-on world.

First, and perhaps most often, authenticity is thought of as being real, or as the Merriam-Webster dictionary puts it, "not false or imitation." In this sense, being authentic means not misrepresenting one's self, being true in word and action at all times. This is, of course, a great sticking point in the digital age. With the ability to create and re-create virtual identities using limitless tools and personality profiles, it can be hard to know who's being real and how often. For example, we can Photoshop our pictures to refine, clean up, exaggerate, or even build something that was never there. But more importantly we can

"Photoshop" our online identities, creating and re-creating our self-portraits to suit our fancy (or what we think others would fancy). We can maintain one identity on YouTube and another on Twitter, one on Facebook and another on Second Life—each with their own set of relationships and codes of conduct.

Even if these separate identities are really just splinters of our actual selves, it can be difficult to know who we're dealing with and how to respond.

In extreme cases the results are disastrous, as in the famous case of thirteen-year-old Megan Meier. Meier hanged herself after being verbally harassed by someone on MySpace who had created a fake identity known as "Josh Evans." The account that was used to produce the fake identity was difficult to trace—many people had access to it and it was not immediately clear who was responsible. As Tim Barker, reporting for the *St. Louis Post-Dispatch*, wrote, "Local authorities declined to file charges, saying the circumstances—various people had access to the account—made it difficult to assign blame. Creating the fictional Josh Evans, Megan's tormentor, was not considered a crime." Fortunately a case like Meier's is extremely rare (though, according to the research, the practice of "cyber-bullying"—in the form of harassment via email, Web sites, and text messages—continues to grow[2]).

For the most part our inaccurate or incomplete forms of self-presentation are quite harmless. "It's just so much easier to pretend to be someone else online. People are very eager to try

2 For more information, visit www.stopcyberbullying.org.

it out," said David Whittier, a professor of education at Boston University. Whittier conceded that obviously things "went too far" in the Meier case, but that for the most part, acting out of virtual identities is more good or neutral than bad. "There's really nothing wrong with [being someone else online]. In a way, it's a wonderful thing." The habit of being someone else online provokes a number of questions in regard to regulation, none of which have any easy answers. When asked by Barker whether the Internet can be regulated in such a way that would facilitate more online honesty, Catherine Dwyer, a professor at Pace University's Seidenberg School of Computer Science and Information Systems, said she doubts it. "Imagine the difficulties of forcing every online user to prove their identity when signing up for sites like MySpace. None of us want to live in a world where you have to be authenticated all of the time." Dwyer's comment might give us pause to ask: Where does authenticity fit in a world where we refuse to be authenticated?

Jesus demonstrated that the safe space needed for a human relationship to thrive had to be rooted in honesty. Without honesty, there can be no trust. And without trust, there can be no intimacy. That's why early in Jesus' conversation with the Samaritan woman, He invited her to relate to Him in open and honest terms ("You are right when you say you have no husband"). But He also demonstrated great respect for the woman's personal information, never using it against her to create an artificial intimacy the way we often do online. Such is the case when we assume to know a person because we know a number of technical details about their lives (where they work, when they were born, what their family looks like, where they most recently went for vacation).

Because of the depersonalizing effect mentioned above, we often feel less inhibited in how we interact with one another online, especially in terms of what kind of personal information we share. As a result it becomes easy to overshare ourselves, to reveal more information—or information at a faster rate—than we would face-to-face (after all, we wouldn't normally think of sharing the volume and depth of personal information in a first meeting like we do on the average Facebook profile). Our tendency toward oversharing can be an attempt to get other people's attention. At its worst it is a form of emotional pornography—we get the brief and intense feeling of intimacy without having to worry about commitment, conflict resolution, or the time required to build a truly intimate relationship. This pattern of oversharing does not promote intimacy. Rather, we're just getting "our stuff" out of our system so that we feel better. Oversharing does not take into account the thoughts and feelings of the other person. But it does give the impression that we know each other much better than we actually do and this, again, is one of the challenges in relating authentically to one another online.

The temptation to misrepresent ourselves on sites like Facebook is the issue that gets the most press, stirring up concern (largely from older users) and controversy among lawmakers who are all trying to answer the question, "What is real?" and, "What are the implications of what's real?" But the "obvious issue" is merely a flashing neon sign pointing toward the deeper issue, and that brings us to the second definition of authenticity.

Authenticity in the second sense has to do with living in accordance to one's true nature. Dr. James Bugental, who wrote *The Search for Authenticity*, said, "By authenticity I mean a central genuineness and awareness of being. Authenticity is difficult to convey in words, but experientially it is readily perceived in ourselves or in others." As if to clarify Bugental's statement that authenticity is best viewed through the lens of experience, psychologist and author Richard Sharf offered the following comparisons between authentic and inauthentic individuals:

> *The values and goals of authentic individuals are very much their own, whereas inauthentic individuals may have goals based on others and be less conscious of what is of importance to them. In social interactions, authentic individuals are oriented toward intimacy, whereas inauthentic individuals are more concerned with superficial relationships. In a broader sense, authentic individuals are concerned about their society and social institutions such as schools and charities, whereas inauthentic individuals are less concerned with them. The authentic person experiences existential anxiety over issues related to freedom, responsibility, death, isolation, and meaning. In contrast, the inauthentic individual experiences guilt about having missed opportunities, as well*

as cowardice because she has not had the courage to change or make risky decisions. Whereas the authentic person may experience existential crises that produce anxiety, the inauthentic individual is more likely to experience psychopathology and maladaptive means of dealing with crises.

Authenticity defined in these terms means that *what we do* springs out of *who we are*. And this naturally leads to the question, "Who are we?"

As Bugental says, "We can see who we really are—in our words and actions—better than we can describe it." Therefore our true nature—that is, our nature that reflects the image of God—is naturally oriented toward personal responsibility. It is naturally oriented toward intimacy. It is naturally oriented toward caring for the needs of others. It is naturally oriented toward working hard for what matters most. As a result, when we think, speak, and act from our true nature, we will always be a benefit to others while reaping benefit for ourselves. Conversely we can know that whenever we choose to act carelessly, choose to relate superficially, choose to avoid the difficult stuff in life merely because it's uncomfortable, we are not living out of our true nature. Instead we are being inauthentic. And while authentic living naturally generates new clarity and freedom, inauthentic living naturally creates confusion and emotional captivity. "If we are unfaithful to true self," says Parker Palmer, "we will extract a price from others. We will make promises we cannot keep, build houses from flimsy stuff, conjure dreams that devolve into nightmares, and other people will suffer." Jesus' conversation with the Samaritan woman was a natural extension of His character. It was not in Jesus' true nature to do *anything other* than offer life to a person His culture despised. When we live authentically—in congruence with our true nature—we are empowered to offer life to one another, as well.

In the introduction to this book, I asked you to imagine taking a walk across London's Millennium Bridge. When you arrived at the south bank of the Thames, you found yourself standing in front of the Tate Modern Art Gallery, pleased that admission was free (after all, you were on a budget). I described it as looking like a giant industrial barn where one might milk several thousand cows, and I wasn't too far off. As it turns out, the Tate Modern is actually built from the shell of a large abandoned power station.

The Tate Modern is one of four related art galleries that include the Tate Britain, the Tate Liverpool, and the Tate St. Ives. By 1990 it was clear that the other three were bulging at the seams, housing the entire national art collection from 1500 forward and including a large international collection. A new space was needed to share the load, and the decision was made to create a London gallery specifically for modern art (i.e., art created anywhere from 1900 to the present day). The immediate concern was: Should it be a new building or the conversion of an existing structure? After a long and thorough search, it was determined that the former power station sitting across the Thames from St. Paul's Cathedral would be perfect for converting into a hip art gallery. It was big, it already had an architectural uniqueness (it looked like a large abandoned power station), and, most importantly, it was available (it had closed in 1982). The search committee was thrilled in an understated British way, and immediately started an international search for the new gallery's architects. Simultaneously a discussion began around the possibility of a new footbridge that would link the north and south banks of the Thames. Hmm, thought the search committee, that could be a nice touch.

An old power station is an ideal structure for an art gallery because it offers plenty of space. In its original form the building housed a massive turbine that took up most of that space. The turbine was removed, and now at 150 feet high and 450 feet long, the main Turbine Hall looks something like a massive airline terminal. The boiler house that ran along the length of the Hall was also converted. In its new form the Boiler House has three levels—the first two contain permanent art collections and the third houses rotating exhibitions. On top of the main building sits a two-story glass penthouse that houses a cafe and looks out over the city of London. And perhaps most notable upon first glance, a giant chimney stack towers over the whole structure.

Since it's opening in 2000, the Tate Modern has received more than thirty million visitors, making it the third most popular tourist attraction in the UK.[3] Its only problem is that it is too popular. The original design was intended to support about 1.8 million visitors a year, but in recent years, that number has soared to 4.6 million people annually. The Tate Modern's facilities are straining under the unprecedented traffic. Apparently even a large abandoned power station has its limits. What to do?

In late March 2009 plans were approved for the Tate Modern 2, a radical half-pyramid, half-rectangle structure that will attach to one corner of the current Tate Modern like an odd and very visible wart. The TM2, as it's been dubbed, will utilize the original massive oil tanks (now empty) for its foundation, with the remaining structure wrapping up and around them. In addition, the TM2 will contain unique spaces within the massive oil tanks for performance and film, a new children's gallery, spaces for learning and study, dedicated family areas, and more restaurants and cafes. The completion of the TM2 is scheduled to coincide with the 2012 London Olympics and Paralympics, and perhaps best of all, you'll be able to tour most of it for free.

The Tate Modern Gallery is an excellent example of regeneration— of taking something old and making it new, of taking something good and making it better. And now, arriving at the end of our

---

3 The other two most popular tourist destinations in the UK: Buckingham Palace and Victoria Beckham's shoe closet. I'm just kidding—no one goes to Buckingham Palace anymore.

exploration of Facebook, it is appropriate to ask, "How can we take our co-creative tools modeled by Jesus—intentionality, humility, and authenticity—and use them to make something good like Facebook even better?"

There are, of course, no easy answers. But that doesn't mean there are no answers at all. In fact there are a number of ways we can begin practicing intentionality, humility, and authenticity in our hyperconnected context right now. The following is a brief list to get us thinking and moving.

1. Practice regular check-ins.

Much of our lives can be an out-of-body experience, especially when we're busy mindlessly scrolling through Facebook. Check in with yourself throughout the day—whatever you're doing— and do a quick personal inventory. What am I feeling right now? What kinds of thoughts are going through my head in this moment? For example, immediately after getting a work email, you might ask yourself what kinds of thoughts and emotions it surfaced. Did it make you anxious? Are you second-guessing how you should reply? Are you ambivalent, annoyed, thrilled? Don't worry about what the email means for the rest of your day, week, *life*. Just focus your attention on what kinds of thoughts and feelings are flitting through your mind right here and now. Learning to regularly check in with ourselves this way trains our brains to be mindful and puts us back in touch with our bodies.

We can only exist in the present moment, and mindful living helps us find our way back to the present.

2. Make the intention to not go online immediately before bed and immediately after waking up.

Give yourself space at the beginning and the end of your day to focus your attention in the present moment as a way of unplugging and coming back to yourself. One way of doing this would be to memorize a short psalm or other passage from Scripture (Psalm 23 is a good place to start). Right after you wake up and before you get out of bed, thoughtfully recite the prayer in your mind once or twice, then say a short prayer inviting God into the details of your day. At night, after climbing into bed and before falling asleep, take a few moments to recall your day and pick out three things you can genuinely be thankful for. Thank God for them in prayer and commit your night's sleep to Him, as well, trusting that the same God who is attentive and working while you're asleep can more than handle the details of your to-do list.

3. Practice mindful Facebooking.

Make the intention to *pay attention* to how you spend your time on Facebook. How much time of your day does it take up?

It may not look like much initially, but a dozen visits over the course of the day add up. When you're on Facebook, how do you spend your time? Is it keeping in touch with close friends? Is it scanning status updates looking for the most interesting? Is it checking out the provocative pictures your acquaintance-of-an-acquaintance just posted? How does it *feel* to see new pictures, to add a friend, to look for and find old friends? What do you look forward to when you check Facebook? What do you enjoy most about the experience of it? Check in with yourself every now and then right in the middle of your Facebooking and see what's going on in your thoughts and feelings.

4. Practice authentic Facebooking.

Because Facebook is an environment that typically rewards the most clever or the most willing to risk self-revelation, we can sometimes exaggerate or downplay certain things about ourselves to get a response. Likewise, we can be tempted to "overshare" ourselves with others in order to get and/or keep their attention. Obviously most of this is good fun. We can certainly take ourselves too seriously, even in such a playful environment, and that would not help any of us. But many of our relationships are starving for a lack of authentic interaction. One quick way we can practice "authentic Facebooking": Take a look at your profile—the pictures you've posted, the information you've shared. Does the content reflect your God-given nature? Is it "true" to who you really are? If you're funny, be funny. If you're artistic, be artistic. If you're neither, just be you. This can be applied to your interactions with others, too, whether in a wall-post, a message, or a status update. Are you being "you" in the way you interact with your Facebook friends?

5. Adopt one or two Facebook friends for one month.

Most of us have plenty of people in our friends list that we don't necessarily think about or even care that much about. One way our Facebooking can be more intentional (and perhaps more meaningful) is by picking one or two people from our list and focusing our attention on them for thirty days. Find out what's specifically going on in their lives and find ways to encourage them accordingly. Pray for them daily. Send them messages just for them, not for the public to see on their wall. Do you have any fun, flattering pictures from times shared together? Post them on your page and share the link with your friend to celebrate the memory. Invite them to meet in person and share a meal if possible. Do this for one month, then take a quick inventory: Did your intentionality draw you closer? What was it like to focus on one or two friends rather than to try to keep track of several hundred? Did you enjoy it? Was it difficult? By "adopting" one or two people from our friends list for a month, we intentionally engage one another in an environment where intentionality does not have much value (besides marketing and advertising, which are, by far, the most intentional actions on Facebook). The practice of adopting a friend can actually be a practice in humility, as well, as we intentionally seek after the good of someone else, whether or not we get credit for it.

As we saw earlier, the entire story of the Tate Modern Gallery is one of regeneration: An aging trio of old museums birthed a new little brother. An abandoned power plant was transformed into a cutting-edge art gallery. Boiler houses became showcases of creative thought and ingenuity. Oil tanks are being turned into performance spaces. This same thread of regeneration is woven throughout the stories we've discovered in this book. The designers of the Millennium Bridge had to rethink their original design, and in so doing, ended up with one of the most beautiful (and now most stable) suspension bridges in the world. Harlow and his monkeys helped us rethink human nature and discover our great need for a safe space to call "home." Willis Carrier took the simple idea of air-conditioning and transformed geography, architecture, and social structures in the process. Nakeel Properties literally "re-created" the world. Virgil was blind but then could see, and had to submit himself to the difficulty of learning to live in a sighted world. The Hubble Space Telescope extended that seeing deep into space, shifting the way we understand the universe. And Jesus took a woman who was dying of thirst and gave her a drink of water that changed her life.

One of the best things about Facebook is that it continues this regenerative spirit. It is a space where all are invited to participate, to add to the conversation, to share our experiences past and current, to share our hopes and partner in new visions of the future, to reinvent, reclaim, redeem, renew. Facebook is not a perfect environment—there is no such thing. In many ways, we're just beginning to learn how to be human in it. We have the mandate to step in with eyes wide open because it can blur the lines of identity and relationships. So we must work hard to be clear, with ourselves and with one another, but clarity is not impossible.

With intentionality, humility, and authenticity, we can exchange fear-smudged lenses for twenty-twenty vision. We can make intentional movements toward satisfying our longing for "home" by turning our attention toward the quality of both our in-person and online relationships rather than just the quantity. We can humbly recognize the value of every single person in our friends list and treat each person with the respect and dignity he or she deserves. We can authentically express the uniqueness of who we are in ways that are true to our God-reflecting nature and that set the stage for relationships without pretense. In short, we can learn to utilize the brilliant but simple tools in front of us to creatively and joyfully take something good and make it even better.

And with that, all the Church of Facebook said, Amen.

ACKNOWLEDGMENTS

Every book has a story of how it came to be. And a story seems like a good way to say thank you.

My mom, Evelyn Marie Rice (April 26, 1949—January 2, 1997), taught me how to read and instilled in me a love for books that I will always be grateful for. I think she would be very happy to know I actually wrote one. My dad, Gary Rice, the pastor, and my sister, Christin Rice, the San Francisco novelist, nurtured that affection for books while loving me through camping trips, ten family relocations, and more laughter and tears than any one family should enjoy. When my stepmom, the singer, came along, she fit right in (I'm so glad you joined the fun, Mary). Thank you, my dear family, for loving me the way you do.

My wife, Katie, will tell you that I can't remember the day we first met. It's true. But I've rarely forgotten a day since. It was Katie who first helped me believe I might actually have something to say, and it was Katie who wouldn't let anything get in the way of pursuing writing. Thank you for your selflessness through the process of writing this book. You encouraged me from the very beginning, you laughed (and cried) with me in the middle, and you celebrated with me in the end. There's nothing sweeter than wholeheartedly chasing our dreams together.

When I sat down in his office and asked how one goes about writing a book, John Ortberg told me, "You have a good sense of humor—you should pay attention to that. Also, you should write some articles." Thanks for the encouragement and advice, John. When Nancy Ortberg read over one of my articles and then forwarded it on to "a publisher friend" of hers, I was grateful. I still am—thanks, Nancy.

When Don Pape, Nancy's "publisher friend," got the article, he emailed me. Don, your encouragement, advocacy, and shared loved of music has been such a gift. Thanks for believing from the beginning. When Don connected me to Andrea Christian Heinecke, I was given yet another gift—a champion for my book proposal. Thanks, Andrea, for working so hard to turn that proposal into a contract. Thanks, also, to the publishing board at David C. Cook for saying yes. Thanks to Brian Thomasson, Ingrid Beck, and Jaci Schneider and the rest of the David C. Cook family for all their hard work. Thanks, especially, for putting me in touch with the one and only Nicci Jordan Hubert. An author couldn't ask for a better editor. Nicci, you put up with sifting through *two* full manuscripts, an eighteen-hour time difference, a one-second cell phone delay, and too many late nights to count. Your pep talks, insight, and vision—and especially your mad editing skills—made all the difference. Thank you.

Of course, a book has to be written somewhere. Thank you, Hardwin and Tamara Mead, not only for a "treehouse" to write and live in, but also for your faithful friendship. Paul and Heather Grant helped Katie and me spend three months writing, playing music, and studying in Tauranga, New Zealand. Thank you (and everyone at Welcome Bay Community Church) for inviting us to come "down under." Bob and Mary, David and Erin—you have each extended "home" to me. I can't believe I got so lucky.

Scott Scruggs read an early draft and wouldn't let me give up. Scruggs, I'm so thankful for your friendship. Dudley and Penny, you have both played such key roles in helping me become who I am. Thank you for the countless conversations. Last, but certainly not least, I'm grateful to the members of the "I'm Helping Jesse Write A Book!" Facebook group. Your willingness to join in the conversation actually did, in the end, help Jesse write a book.

REFERENCES

Introduction

"Steven Strogatz: How Things in Nature Tend to Sync Up," Steve Stogratz for Ted.com, www.ted.com/index.php/talks/steven_strogatz_on_sync.html (accessed February 2, 2009).

"Millennium Bridge," ARUP Web site, www.arup.com/MillenniumBridge (accessed February 2, 2009).

Steven Stogratz, *Sync: The Emerging Science of Spontaneous Order* (New York: Hyperion, 2003), 1–6.

Chapter One: Connection

Claudia Wallis, "The New Science of Happiness," *Time,* January 9, 2005.

Janet L. Surrey, "Relational Psychotherapy, Relational Mindfulness," in *Mindfulness and Psychotherapy*, eds. Christopher K. Germer, Ronald D. Siegel, Paul R. Fulton (New York: Guilford Press, 2005), 92.

Harry Harlow, "The Nature of Love," *American Psychologist* 13 (1958): 673–85.

"Adoption History: Harry Harlow, Monkey Love Experiments," darkwing.uoregon.edu/~adoption/studies/HarlowMLE.htm (accessed February 5, 2009).

Deborah Blum, *Love At Goon Park* (New York: Basic Books, 2002), 10–30.

"Total Isolation," *Horizon*, BBC 2, (January 22, 2008). www.bbc.co.uk/sn/tvradio/programmes/horizon/broadband/tx/isolation (accessed February 7, 2009).

Henri J.M Nouwen, *Lifesigns* (New York: Doubleday, Image Books Edition, 1990), 28.

"connection," definition #7, Encarta World English Dictionary on Microsoft Word 2004.

Genesis 2:18

Chapter Two: Revolution

"How Air Conditioning Changed America," Old House Web, www.oldhouseweb.com/how-to-advice/how-air-condition-ing-changed-america.shtml (accessed February 9, 2009).

"History of Air Conditioning," Bucknell University Web site, www.facstaff.bucknell.edu/mvigeant/therm_1/AC_final/ bg.htm (accessed February 9, 2009).

Malcolm Jones Jr., "Air Conditioning," *Newsweek*, Winter 1997.

"Record 29,000 Apply to Harvard for Fall," Associated Press for MSNBC, www.msnbc.msn.com/id/28776903 (accessed February 21, 2009).

"The Face Behind Facebook," *60 Minutes*, CBS (January 13, 2008).

Jessi Hempel, "How Facebook Is Taking Over Our Lives," *Fortune*, February 19, 2009.

Ellen McGirt, "Facebook's Mark Zuckerberg: Hacker, Drop Out, CEO," FastCompany.com, December 19, 2007.

David Kirkpatrick, "Facebook's Plan to Hook Up the World," *Fortune*, May 29, 2007.

Brad Stone, "Is Facebook Growing Up Too Fast?" *New York Times*, March 29, 2009.

"Sheryl Sandberg on Facebook's Future," BusinessWeek.com, www.businessweek.com/technology/content/apr2009/ tc2009048_429871_page_2.htm (accessed April 10, 2009).

Statistics from Facebook.com (accessed March 13, 2009).

Linda Marse, "Space to Soothe the Psyche," *Los Angeles Times*, March 8, 2007.

"Raymond De Young Homepage," Staff page at University of Michigan Web site, www-personal.umich.edu/~rdeyoung. (accessed March 14, 2009).

"Christmas Truce of 1914," History.com, www.history.com/ content/christmas/christmas-truce-of-1914 (accessed March 15, 2009).

Dean H. Shapiro Jr., Carolyn E. Schwartz, John A. Astin, "Controlling Ourselves, Controlling Our World," *American Psychologist*: Col. 51, No. 12 (December 1996): 1213-30.

I'm also grateful to Justin Smith at www.insidefacebook.com for his friendship and his trustworthy insight into all things Facebook.

Chapter Three: Dispensation

"The Palm Trilogy," The Palm Web site, www.thepalm.ae (accessed March 19, 2009).

"Where Vision Inspires Humanity," Nakheel Properties Web site, www.nakheel.com (accessed March 19, 2009).

"The World," The World Islands Web site, www.theworld.ae (accessed March 9, 2009).

"Culture and Heritage," Government of Dubai Web site, www.dubaitourism.ae/CultureHeritage/CultureHeritage/ tabid/60/language/en-US/Default.aspx (accessed March 19, 2009).

Douglas Adams, *The Hitchhiker's Guide to the Galaxy* (New York: Pocket Books, 1979), 114–15.

Christine Rosen, "Virtual Friendship and the New Narcissism," *The New Atlantis,* Summer 2007, 15-31.

"Types of Facebook Pictures," Philip J. Guo's Web site, www. stanford.edu/~pgbovine/index.html (accessed November 12, 2008).

Amy Harmon, "25 Random Tips for the Facebook User," *New York Times,* February 7, 2009.

"Overview," B. J. Fogg's Web site, www.bjfogg.com (accessed March 24, 2009).

Albert Bandura, "Self-efficacy," *Encyclopedia of Human Behavior,* Vol. 4, 71–81.

Roy H. Williams III, *Does Your Ad Dog Bite?* (Texas: Miracle Publishing, 1997), 11–19.

Linda Stone, "Continuous Partial Attention—Not the Same as Multi-Tasking," BusinessWeek.com, http://www.businessweek.com/business_at_work/time_management/archives/2008/07/continuous_part.html (accessed April 2, 2009).

Malcolm Gladwell, *The Tipping Point* (New York: Little, Brown, and Company, 2000), 175–81.

Carl Bialik, "Sorry, You Have Gone Over Your Limit of Network Friends," *The Wall Street Journal,* November 16, 2007.

Matthew E. Brashears, Miller McPherson, Lynn Smith-Lovin, "Social Isolation in America," *American Sociological Review*: Vol. 71 (June 2006): 353–75.

Genesis 1:27, 28, 2:15.

Dallas Willard, *The Divine Conspiracy* (San Francisco: HarperCollins, 1998), 21–31.

Chapter Four: Illumination

Oliver Sacks, *An Anthropologist on Mars* (New York: Alfred A. Knopf, Random House, 1995), 108-52.

Danah Boyd, "Taken Out of Context: American Teen Socialty in Networked Publics," dissertation, UC Berkeley, 2008, 158

Brad Stone, "Is Facebook Growing Up Too Fast?" *New York Times*, March 28, 2009.

John Gonzales, "Cold Eagles Sure Are Thin-Skinned," *Philadelphia Inquirer*, March 9, 2009.

Mark Brown, "The Digital Revolution and the Church," *Daystar Magazine*, Jan-Feb 2009.

Lori Aratani, "Kids to Parents: Get out of my Face(book)," *Sydney Morning Herald*, September 1, 2008.

"Reference Check: Is Your Boss Watching?" Information and Privacy Commissioner, Ontario, Canada, 2008.

Andrew Wallenstein, "Why can't Facebook friends accept rejection?" *National Public Radio*, August 7, 2008.

John Berlin, "Head Candy: A Modern Day Romance," *Chicago Tribune*, June 25, 2008.

Proverbs 17:17, 18:24.

Sherry Turkle, "Always-on/Always-on-You: The Tethered Self," in *Handbook of Mobile Communication Studies,* ed. James F. Katz (Cambridge: MIT Press, 2008).

James Surowiecki, *The Wisdom of Crowds* (New York: Anchor Books, 2005).

Jon Kabat-Zinn, *Wherever You Go, There You Are* (New York: Hyperion, 1994), introduction, xv.

Chapter Five: Adaptation

Douglas Adams, *The Hitchhiker's Guide to the Galaxy* (New York: Pocket Books, 1979), 76.

"Out of the Ordinary, Out of this World," NASA Web site, www.hubblesite.org (accessed April 1, 2009).

Bill Bryson, *A Short History of Nearly Everything* (New York: Broadway Books, 2004).

"Spitzer Space Telescope," Spitzer/Caltech Web site, www.spitzer.caltech.edu (accessed April 1, 2009).

"Spacewalkers: The Ultimate High-Wire Act," directed by Bill Einreinhofer, Discovery Channel (April 20, 2000).

Craig Freudenrich, Sarah Kammersgard, "How Hubble Space Telescope Works," HowStuffWorks.com, fall 2008.

Marcia Dunn, "Astronauts Try to Save Hubble Telescope," RedOrbit.com, March 18, 2004.

Dennis Overbye, "Dark, Perhaps Forever," *New York Times*, June 3, 2008.

Robert R. Caldwell, "Dark Energy," *Physics World,* May 2004.

Shane Hipps, "Video Ur: Shane Hipps at NPC," Out of Ur. http://blog.christianitytoday.com/outofur/archives/2009/02/video_ur_shane.html, posted February 12, 2009 (accessed July 27, 2009). Used by permission.

Scott McKnight, "Scott McNight on Virtual Community," Out of Ur, http://blog.christianitytoday.com/outofur/archives/2009/02/scot_mcknight_o.html, posted February 16, 2009 (accessed July 27, 2009). Used by permission.

Anne Jackson, "The Facebook Fast," Out of Ur, http://blog.christianitytoday.com/outofur/archives/2009/02/the_social_netw.html, posted February 24, 2009 (accessed July 27, 2009). Used by permission.

Shane Hipps, "Shane Hipps on 'Virtual Community' Again," Out of Ur, http://blog.christianitytoday.com/outofur/archives/2009/02/shane_hipps_on.html, posted February 27, 2009 (accessed July 27, 2009). Used by permission.

Mark Scandrette, *Soul Graffiti* (San Francisco: Jossey-Bass, 2007), 45–57.

Kansas, N., Manzey, D. *Space Psychology and Pscyhiatry.* (Springer, 2008).

Eric Hurtgen, "Stepping Into Community: Interview with Dallas Willard," RelevantMagazine.com, www.relevantmagazine.com/features-reviews/god/910 (accessed April 6, 2009).

Chapter Six: Regeneration

John 4:1–42.

Philip Yancey, *The Jesus I Never Knew* (Grand Rapids, MI: Zondervan, 1995), 149.

N.T. Wright, *The Challenge of Jesus* (Downer's Grove, IL: InterVarsity Press, 1999), 174–97.

Jon Kabat-Zinn, *Wherever You Go, There You Are* (New York: Hyperion, 1994), 3–7.

Dallas Willard, *The Renovation of the Heart* (Colorado Springs, CO: NavPress, 2002), 88–89.

Romans 7:19–20.

Keith O'Brien, "Calling a technology time out," *Boston Globe,* March 10, 2008.

Bruna Martinuzzi, "Humility: The most beautiful word in the English Language," MindTools.com (accessed April 7, 2009).

Marshall Rosenberg, *Nonviolent Communication* (Encinitas, CA: PuddleDancer Press, 2005), 15–24.

"Authenticity." Definition from Merriam-Webster Dictionary.

Christine Rosen, "Virtual Friendship and the New Narcissism," *The New Atlantis*, Summer 2007, 15–31.

Tim Barker, "Is lying on Facebook, MySpace pages going to become illegal?" *St. Louis Post-Dispatch*, January 20, 2008.

James Bugental, *The Search for Authenticity* (New York: Irvington Publishers, 1988).

Richard Sharf, *Theories of Psychology and Counseling* (Brooks/Cole, 2004), 157–83.

Parker Palmer, *Let Your Life Speak* (San Francisco: Jossey-Bass, 2000), 31

"Tate Modern," Tate Modern Gallery Web site, www.tate.org.uk/modern. (accessed April 9, 2009).

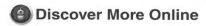**Discover More Online**

CHURCHOFFACEBOOK.COM

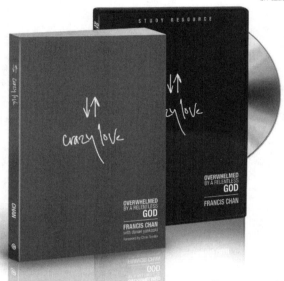